nickelodeon

降世神通

AVATAR

THE LAST AIRBENDER

AVATAR
THE LAST AIRBENDER

SUKI, ALONE

Script
FAITH ERIN HICKS

Art
PETER WARTMAN

Colors
ADELE MATERA

Lettering
**RICHARD STARKINGS &
COMICRAFT'S JIMMY BETANCOURT**

DARK HORSE BOOKS

president and publisher
MIKE RICHARDSON

editor
RACHEL ROBERTS

assistant editor
JENNY BLENK

collection designer
SARAH TERRY

digital art technician
SAMANTHA HUMMER

martial arts consultant and model
TODD BALTHAZOR

Special thanks to Linda Lee, James Salerno, and Joan Hilty at Nickelodeon, to Dave Marshall at Dark Horse, and to Bryan Konietzko, Michael Dante DiMartino, and Tim Hedrick.

Nickelodeon Avatar: The Last Airbender™—Suki, Alone

Published by **Dark Horse Books**
A division of **Dark Horse Comics LLC**
10956 SE Main Street | Milwaukie, OR 97222

DarkHorse.com
Nick.com

To find a comics shop in your area,
visit ComicShopLocator.com

First edition: July 2021
eBOOK ISBN 978-1-50671-716-6 | ISBN 978-1-50671-713-5

3 5 7 9 10 8 6 4 2
Printed in China

MIX
Paper from responsible sources
FSC® C109093
www.fsc.org

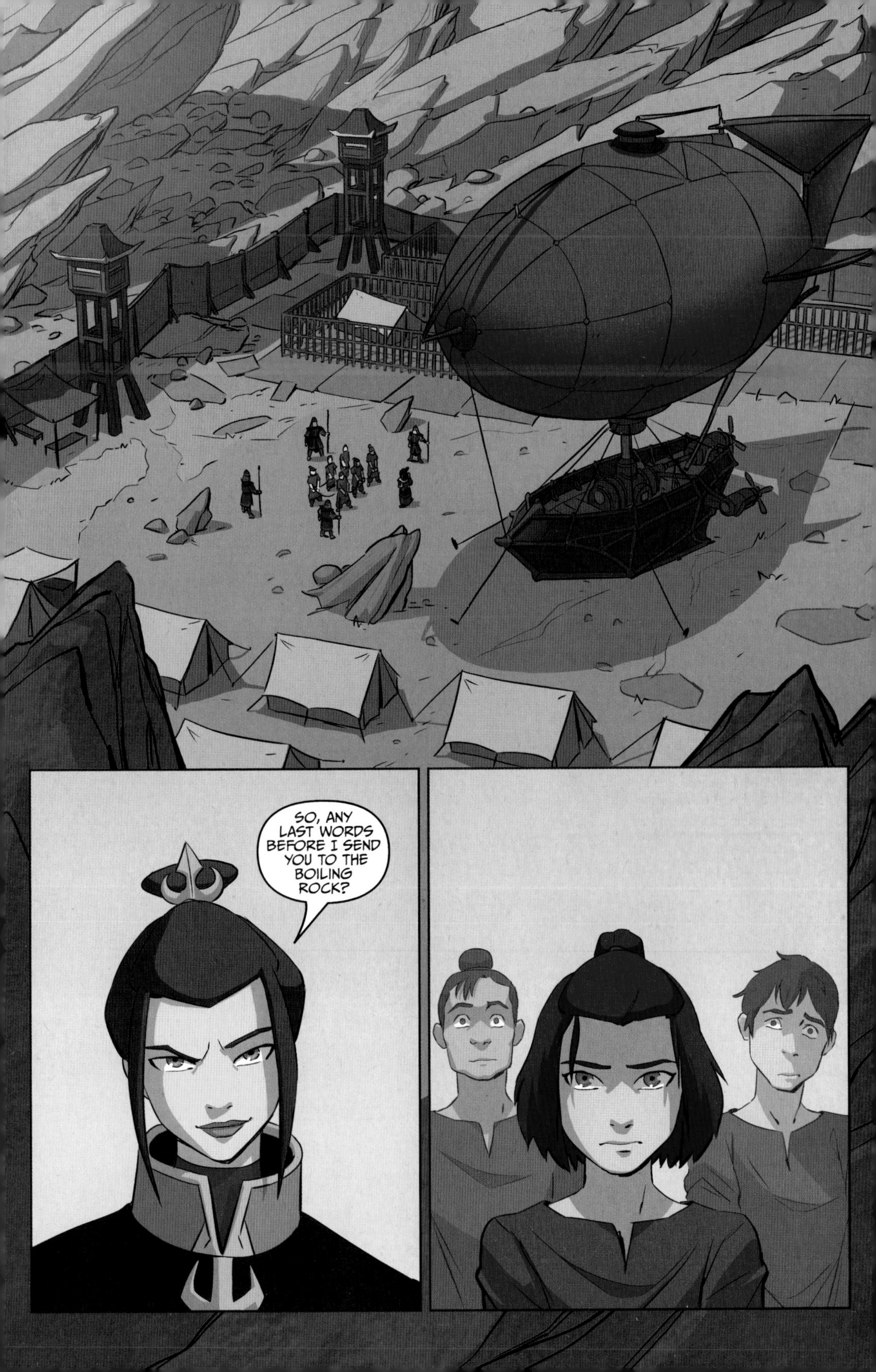
SO, ANY LAST WORDS BEFORE I SEND YOU TO THE BOILING ROCK?

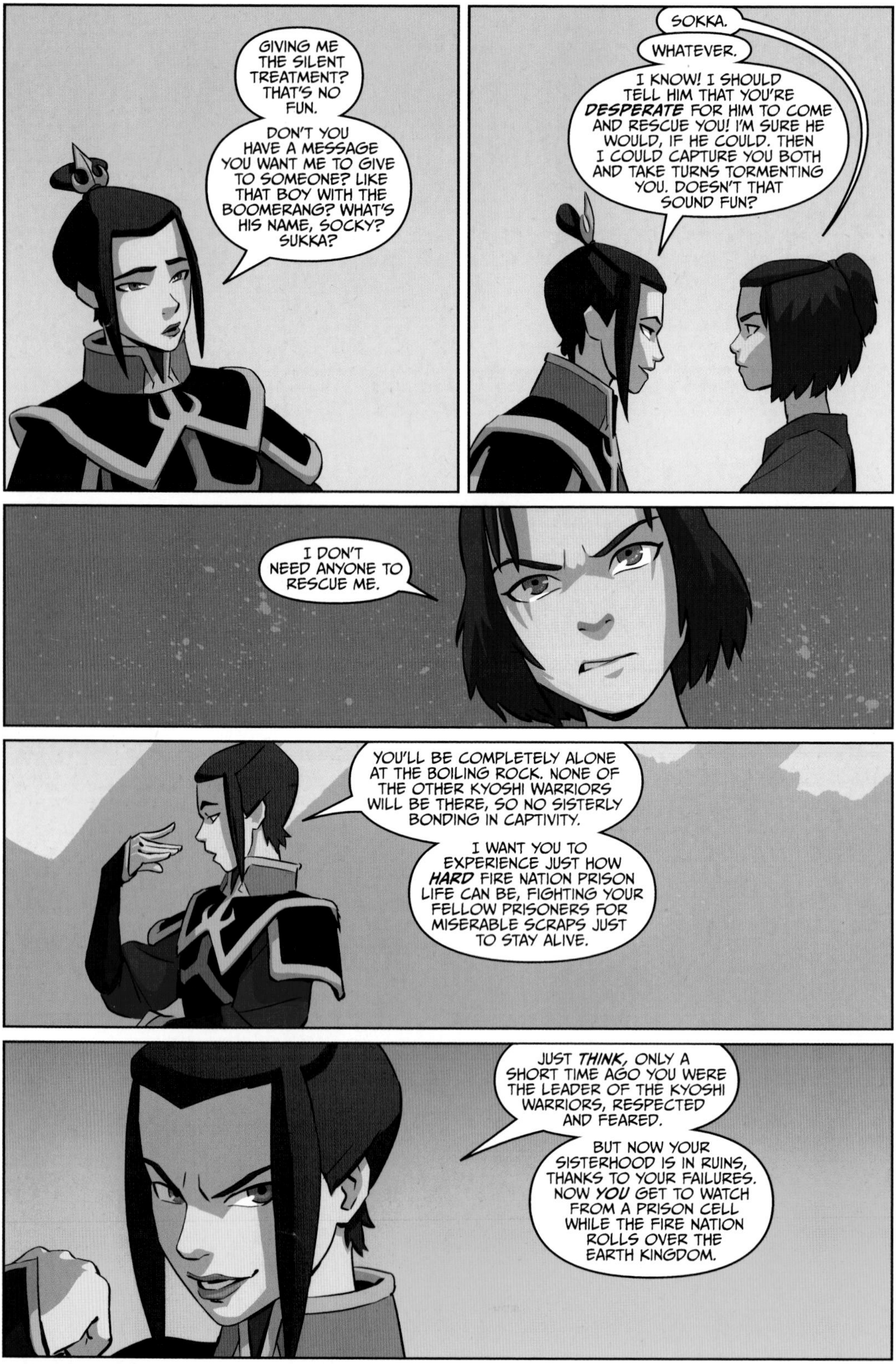
GIVING ME THE SILENT TREATMENT? THAT'S NO FUN.
DON'T YOU HAVE A MESSAGE YOU WANT ME TO GIVE TO SOMEONE? LIKE THAT BOY WITH THE BOOMERANG? WHAT'S HIS NAME, SOCKY? SUKKA?
SOKKA.
WHATEVER.
I KNOW! I SHOULD TELL HIM THAT YOU'RE *DESPERATE* FOR HIM TO COME AND RESCUE YOU! I'M SURE HE WOULD, IF HE COULD. THEN I COULD CAPTURE YOU BOTH AND TAKE TURNS TORMENTING YOU. DOESN'T THAT SOUND FUN?
I DON'T NEED ANYONE TO RESCUE ME.
YOU'LL BE COMPLETELY ALONE AT THE BOILING ROCK. NONE OF THE OTHER KYOSHI WARRIORS WILL BE THERE, SO NO SISTERLY BONDING IN CAPTIVITY.
I WANT YOU TO EXPERIENCE JUST HOW *HARD* FIRE NATION PRISON LIFE CAN BE, FIGHTING YOUR FELLOW PRISONERS FOR MISERABLE SCRAPS JUST TO STAY ALIVE.
JUST *THINK,* ONLY A SHORT TIME AGO YOU WERE THE LEADER OF THE KYOSHI WARRIORS, RESPECTED AND FEARED.
BUT NOW YOUR SISTERHOOD IS IN RUINS, THANKS TO YOUR FAILURES. NOW *YOU* GET TO WATCH FROM A PRISON CELL WHILE THE FIRE NATION ROLLS OVER THE EARTH KINGDOM.

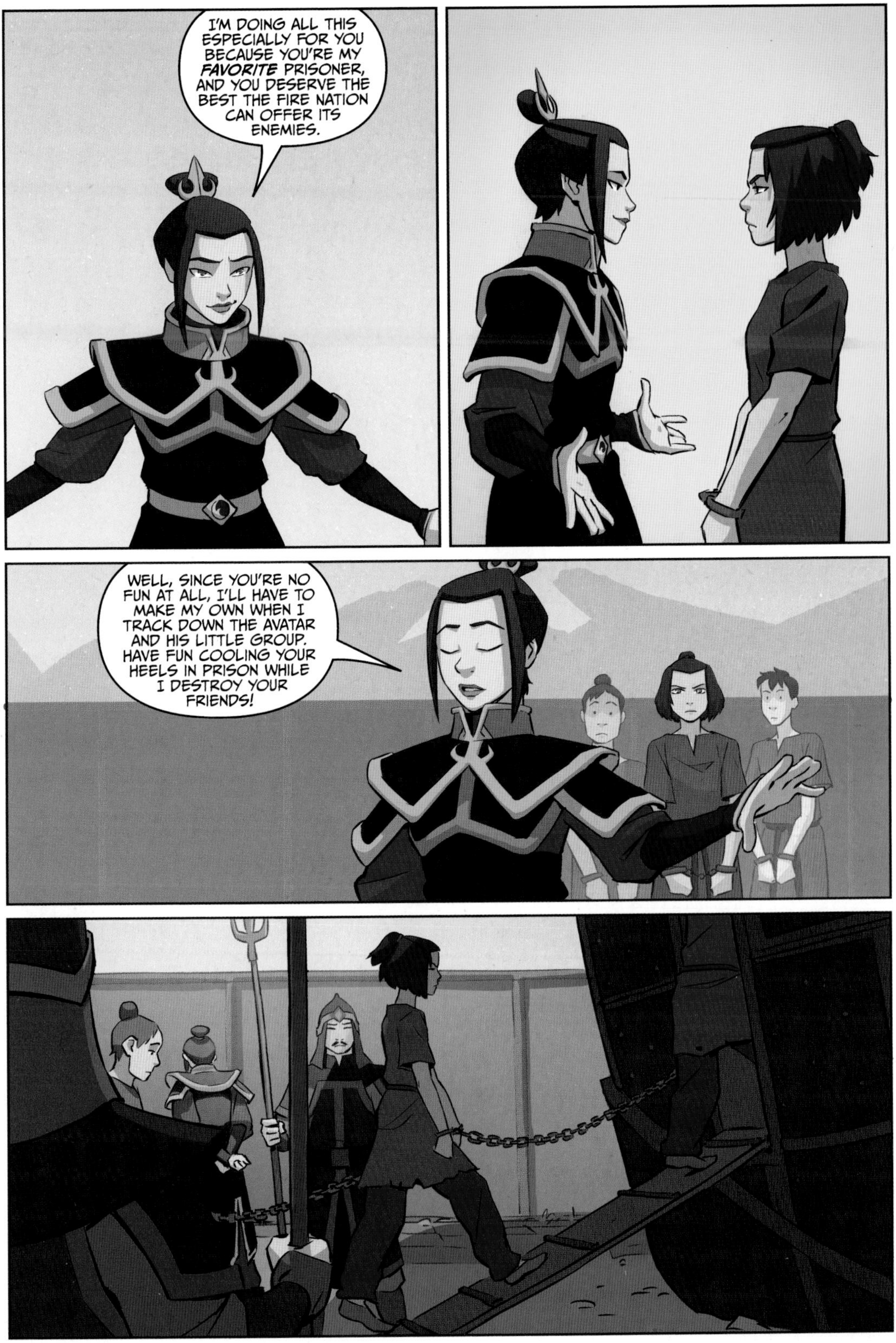

I'M DOING ALL THIS ESPECIALLY FOR YOU BECAUSE YOU'RE MY *FAVORITE* PRISONER, AND YOU DESERVE THE BEST THE FIRE NATION CAN OFFER ITS ENEMIES.
WELL, SINCE YOU'RE NO FUN AT ALL, I'LL HAVE TO MAKE MY OWN WHEN I TRACK DOWN THE AVATAR AND HIS LITTLE GROUP. HAVE FUN COOLING YOUR HEELS IN PRISON WHILE I DESTROY YOUR FRIENDS!

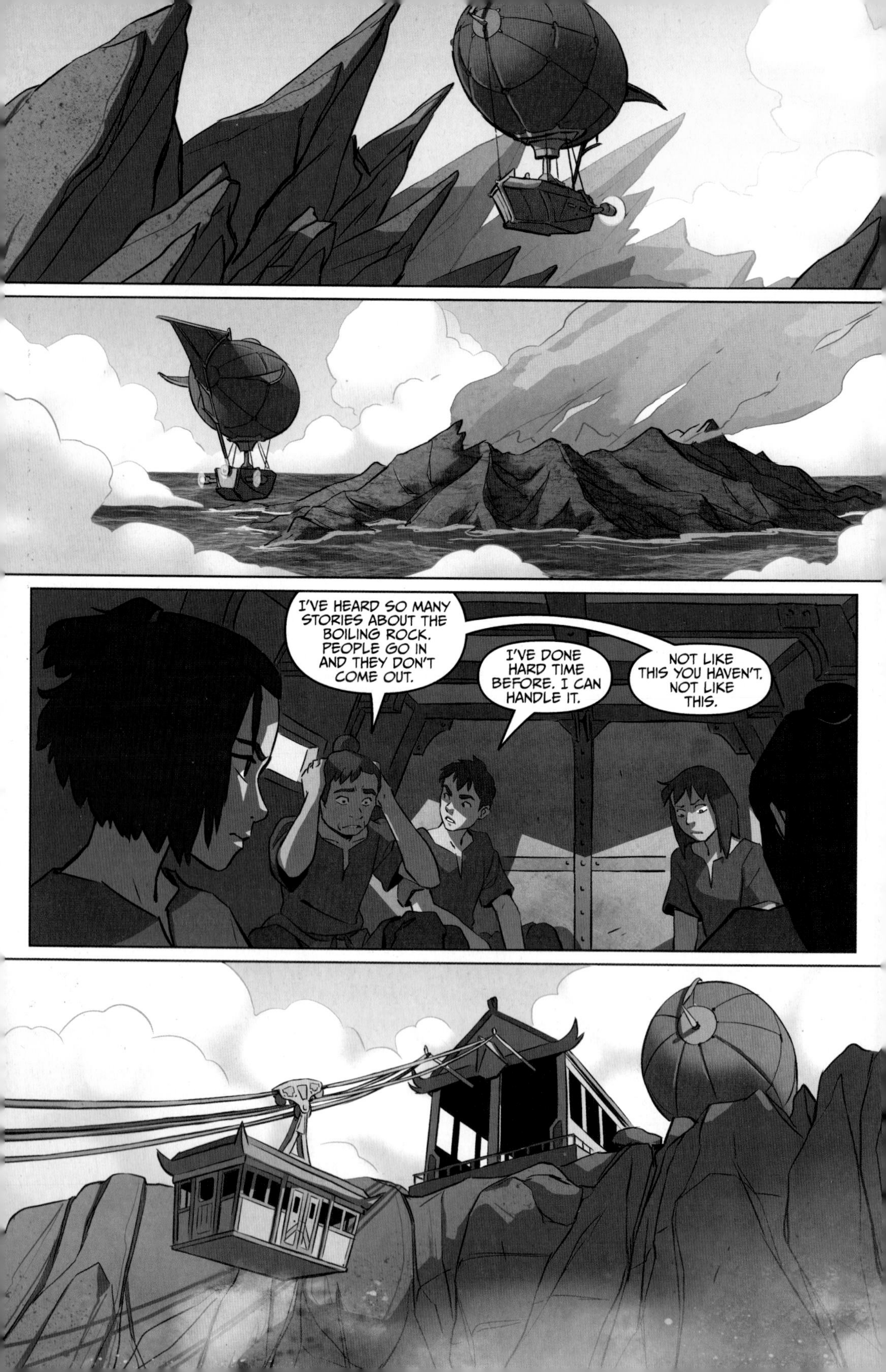
I'VE HEARD SO MANY STORIES ABOUT THE BOILING ROCK. PEOPLE GO IN AND THEY DON'T COME OUT.
I'VE DONE HARD TIME BEFORE. I CAN HANDLE IT.
NOT LIKE THIS YOU HAVEN'T. NOT LIKE THIS.

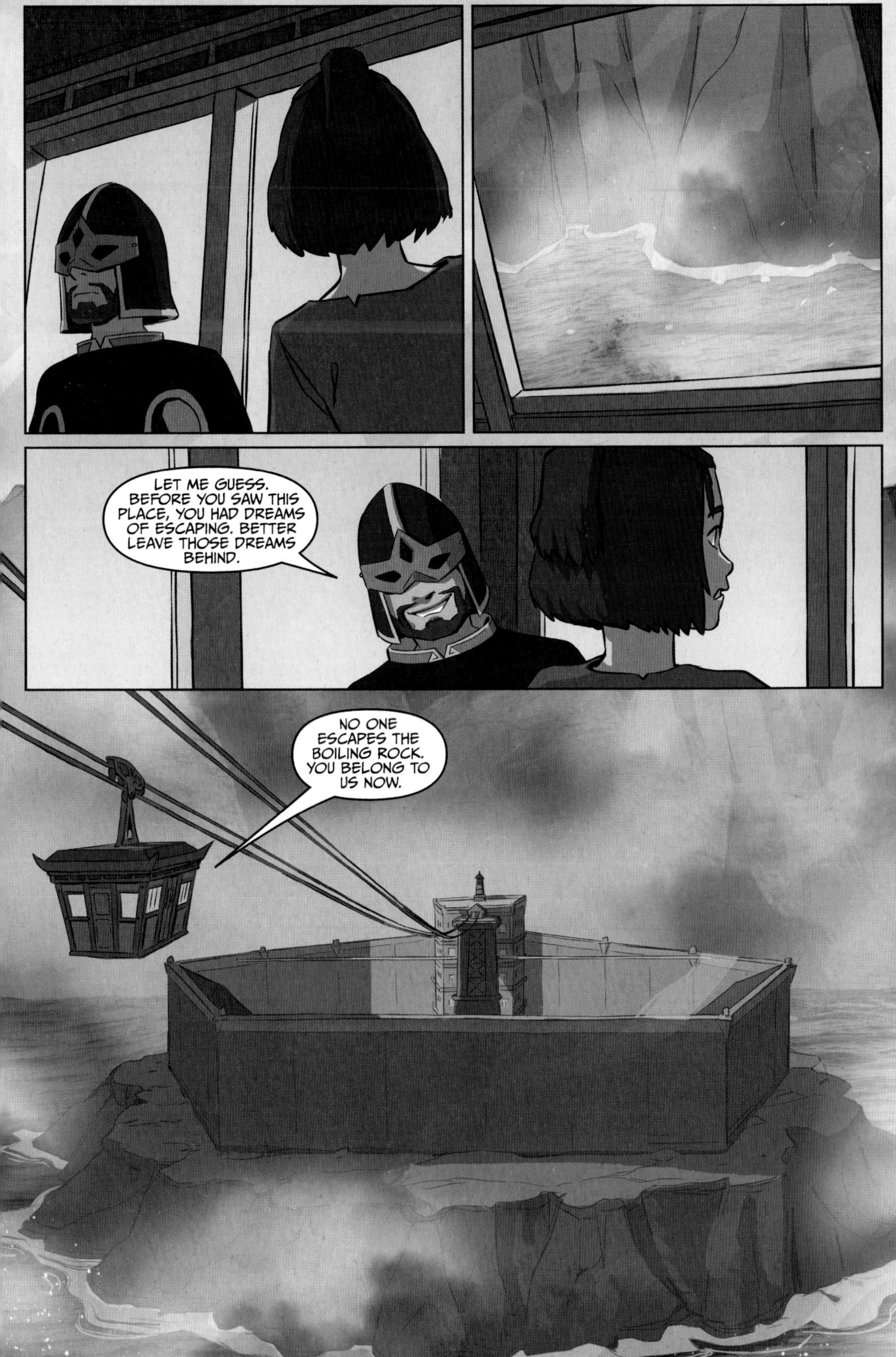
LET ME GUESS. BEFORE YOU SAW THIS PLACE, YOU HAD DREAMS OF ESCAPING. BETTER LEAVE THOSE DREAMS BEHIND.
NO ONE ESCAPES THE BOILING ROCK. YOU BELONG TO US NOW.

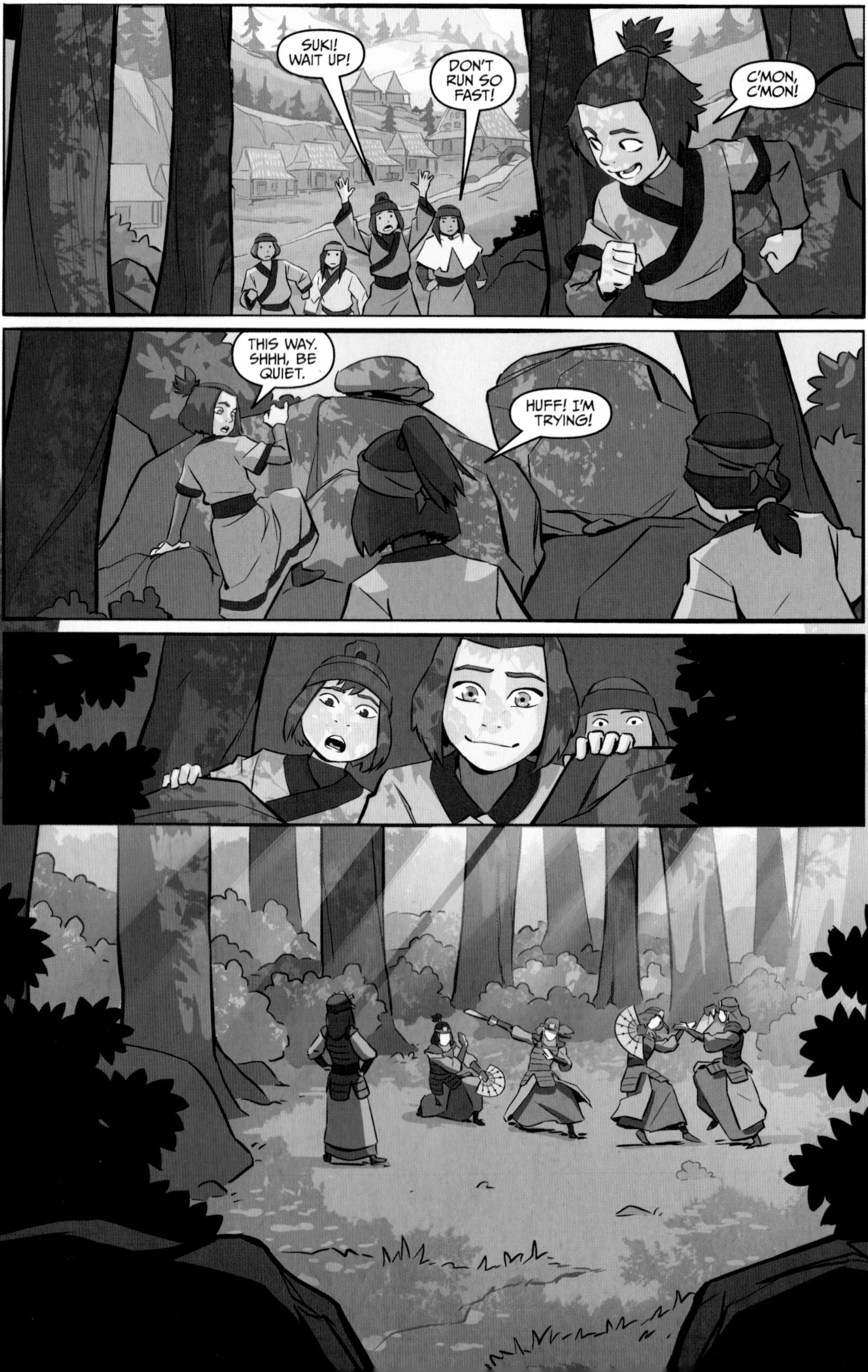
SUKI! WAIT UP!
DON'T RUN SO FAST!
C'MON, C'MON!
THIS WAY. SHHH, BE QUIET.
HUFF! I'M TRYING!

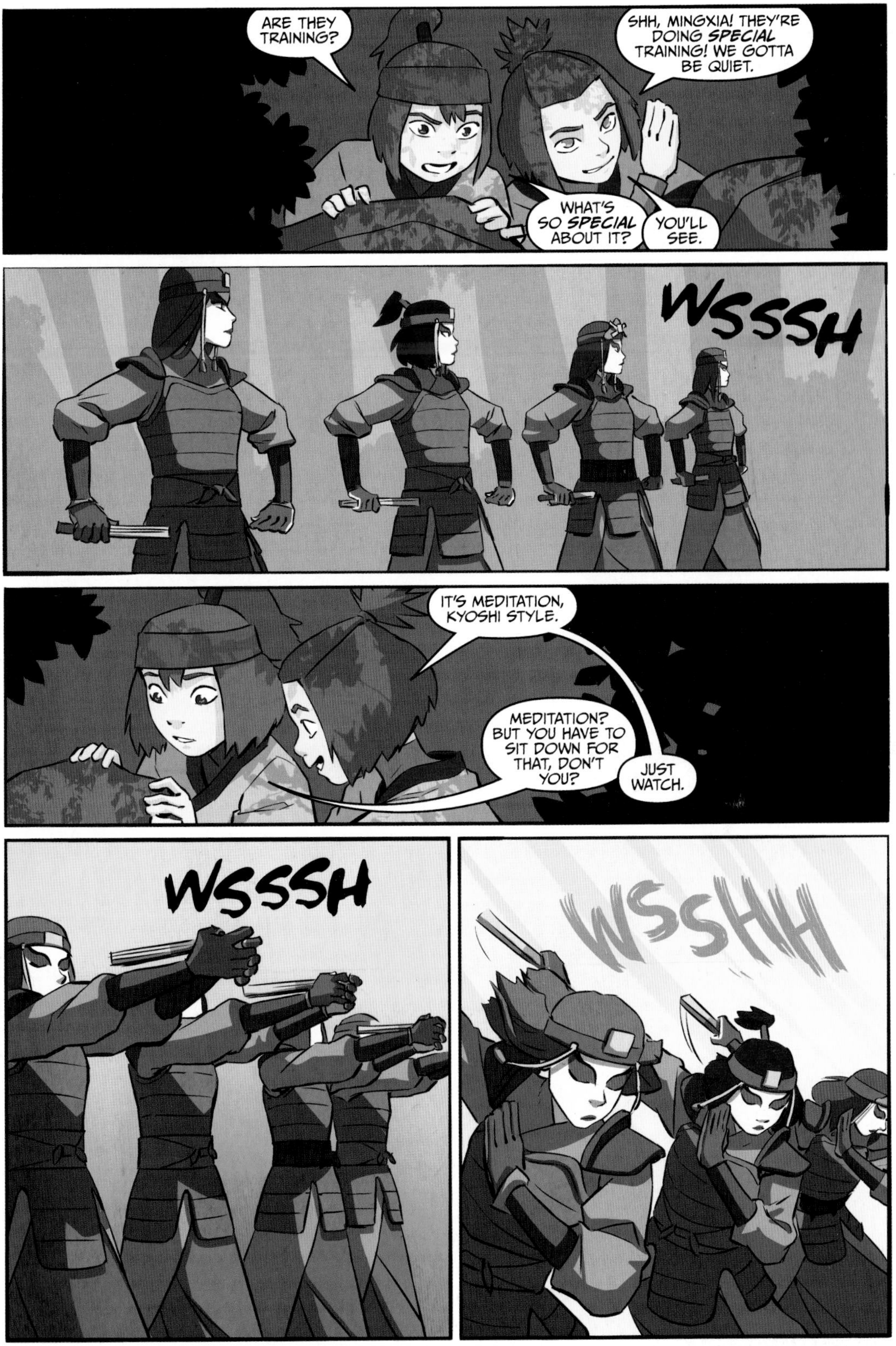
ARE THEY TRAINING?
SHH, MINGXIA! THEY'RE DOING SPECIAL TRAINING! WE GOTTA BE QUIET.
WHAT'S SO SPECIAL ABOUT IT?
YOU'LL SEE.
WSSSH
IT'S MEDITATION, KYOSHI STYLE.
MEDITATION? BUT YOU HAVE TO SIT DOWN FOR THAT, DON'T YOU?
JUST WATCH.
WSSSH
WSSHH

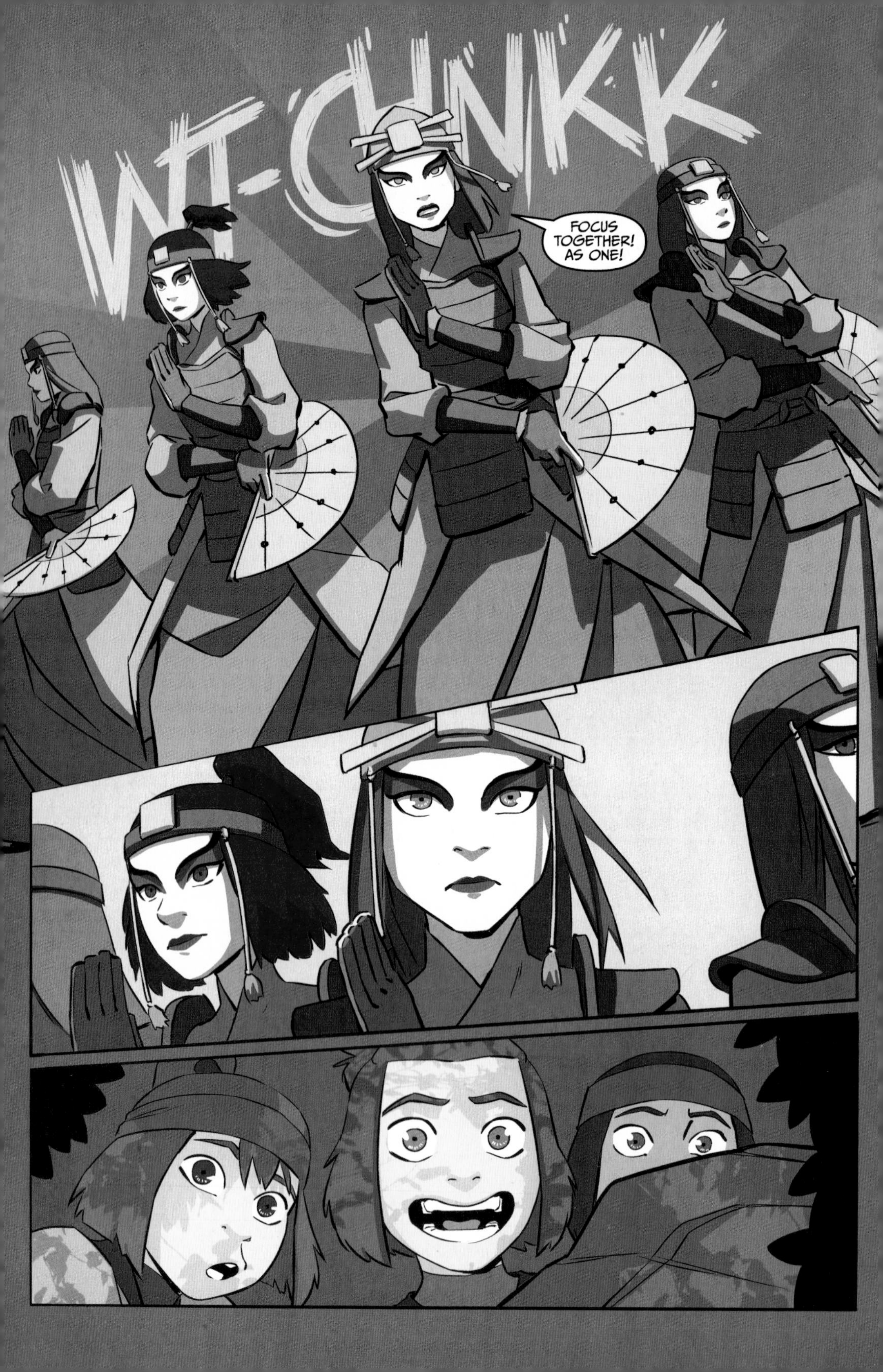
WT-CHNKK
FOCUS TOGETHER! AS ONE!

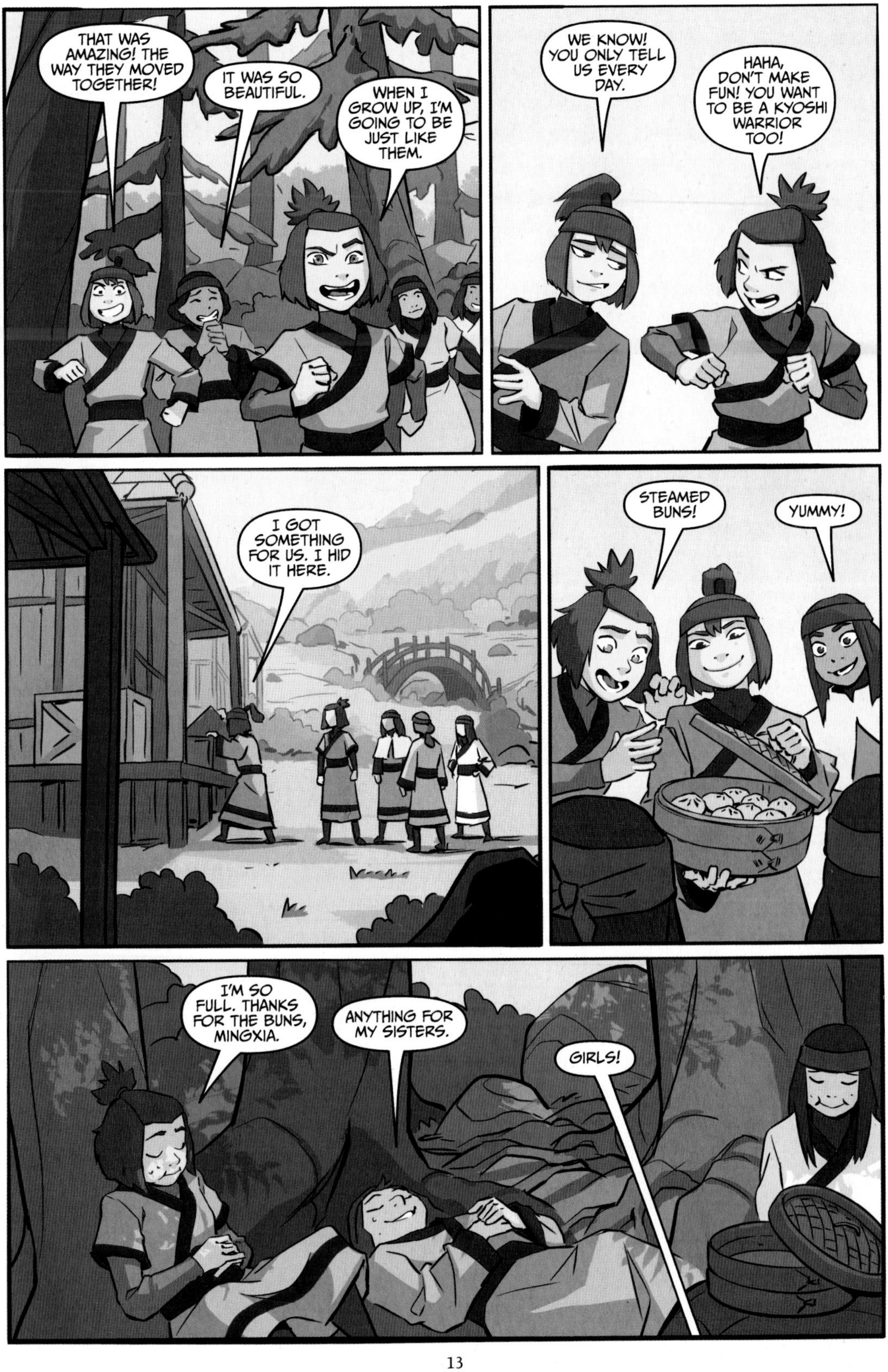
THAT WAS AMAZING! THE WAY THEY MOVED TOGETHER!
IT WAS SO BEAUTIFUL.
WHEN I GROW UP, I'M GOING TO BE JUST LIKE THEM.
WE KNOW! YOU ONLY TELL US EVERY DAY.
HAHA, DON'T MAKE FUN! YOU WANT TO BE A KYOSHI WARRIOR TOO!
I GOT SOMETHING FOR US. I HID IT HERE.
STEAMED BUNS!
YUMMY!
I'M SO FULL. THANKS FOR THE BUNS, MINGXIA.
ANYTHING FOR MY SISTERS.
GIRLS!

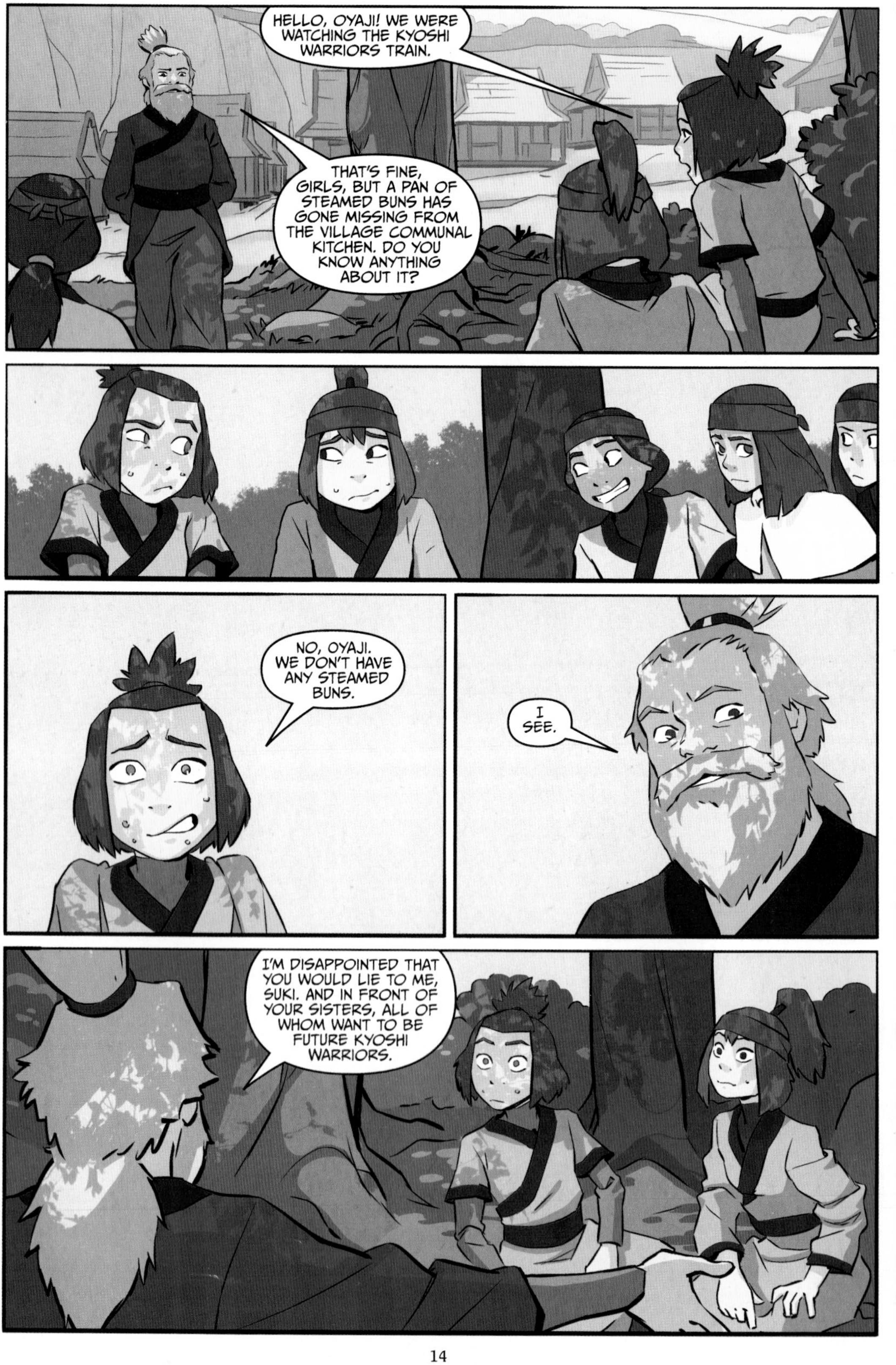
HELLO, OYAJI! WE WERE WATCHING THE KYOSHI WARRIORS TRAIN.
THAT'S FINE, GIRLS, BUT A PAN OF STEAMED BUNS HAS GONE MISSING FROM THE VILLAGE COMMUNAL KITCHEN. DO YOU KNOW ANYTHING ABOUT IT?
NO, OYAJI. WE DON'T HAVE ANY STEAMED BUNS.
I SEE.
I'M DISAPPOINTED THAT YOU WOULD LIE TO ME, SUKI. AND IN FRONT OF YOUR SISTERS, ALL OF WHOM WANT TO BE FUTURE KYOSHI WARRIORS.

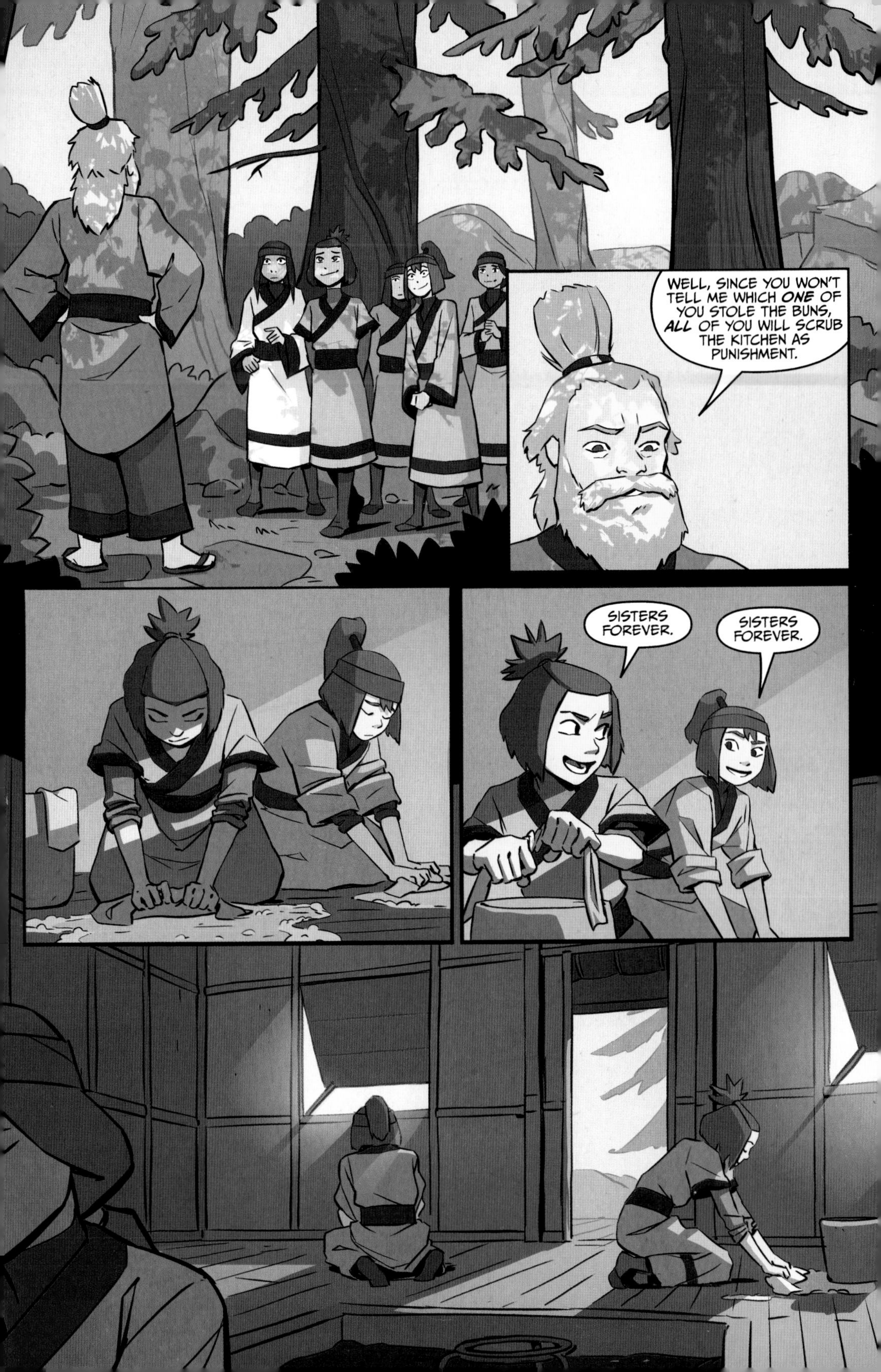
WELL, SINCE YOU WON'T TELL ME WHICH **ONE** OF YOU STOLE THE BUNS, **ALL** OF YOU WILL SCRUB THE KITCHEN AS PUNISHMENT.
SISTERS FOREVER.
SISTERS FOREVER.

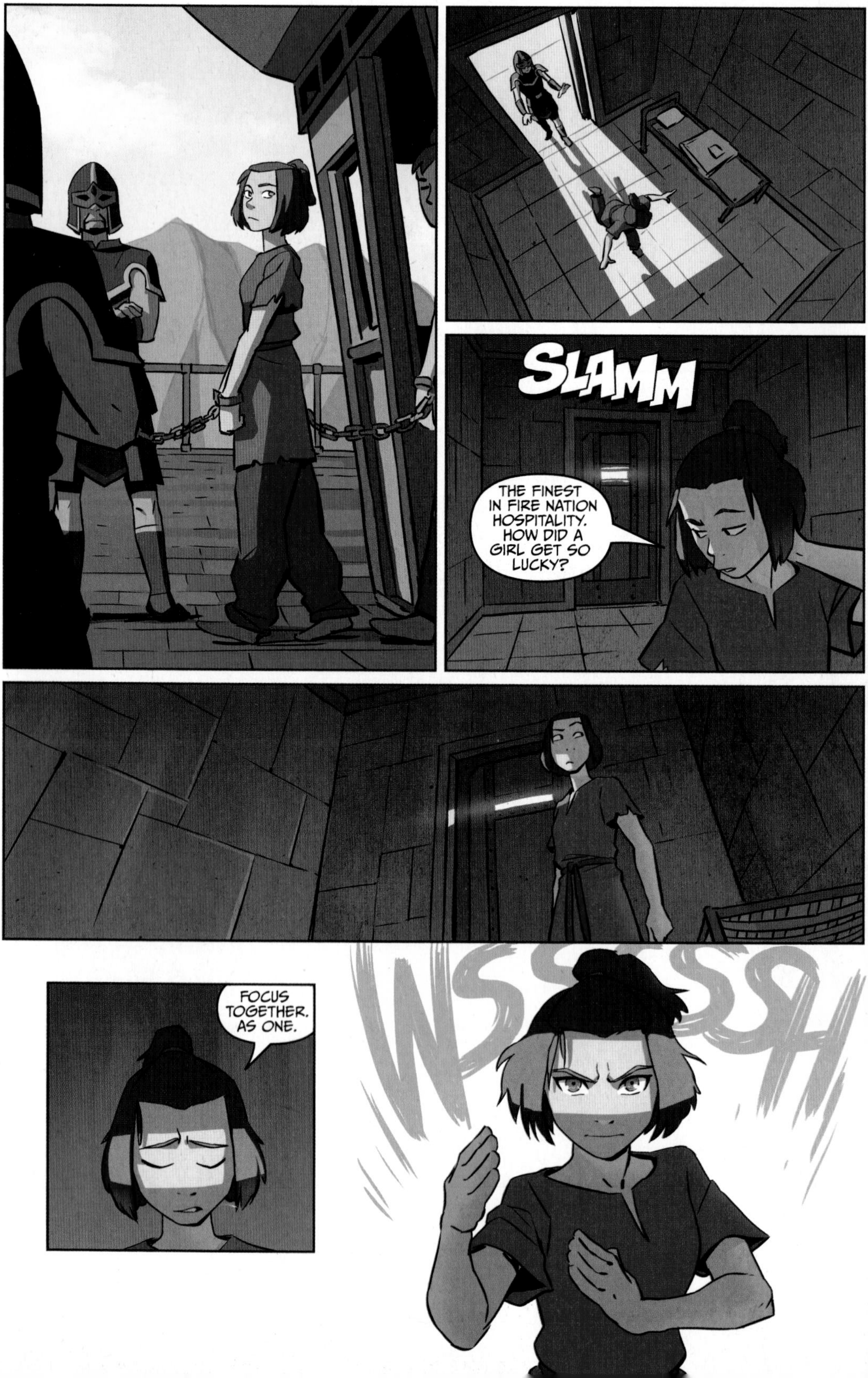
SLAMM
THE FINEST IN FIRE NATION HOSPITALITY. HOW DID A GIRL GET SO LUCKY?
FOCUS TOGETHER. AS ONE.
WSSSSH

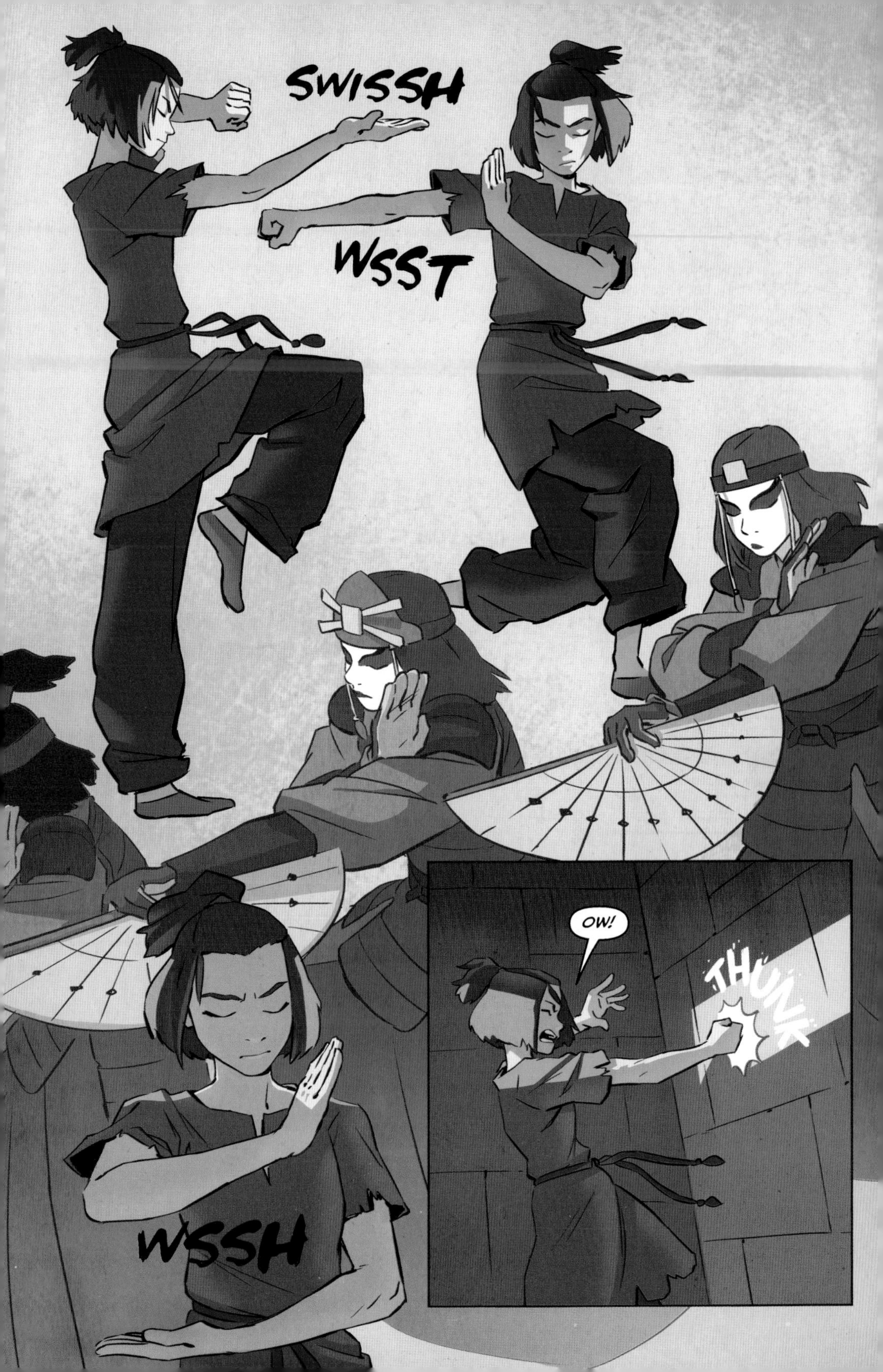
SWISSH
WSST
WSSH
OW!
THUNK

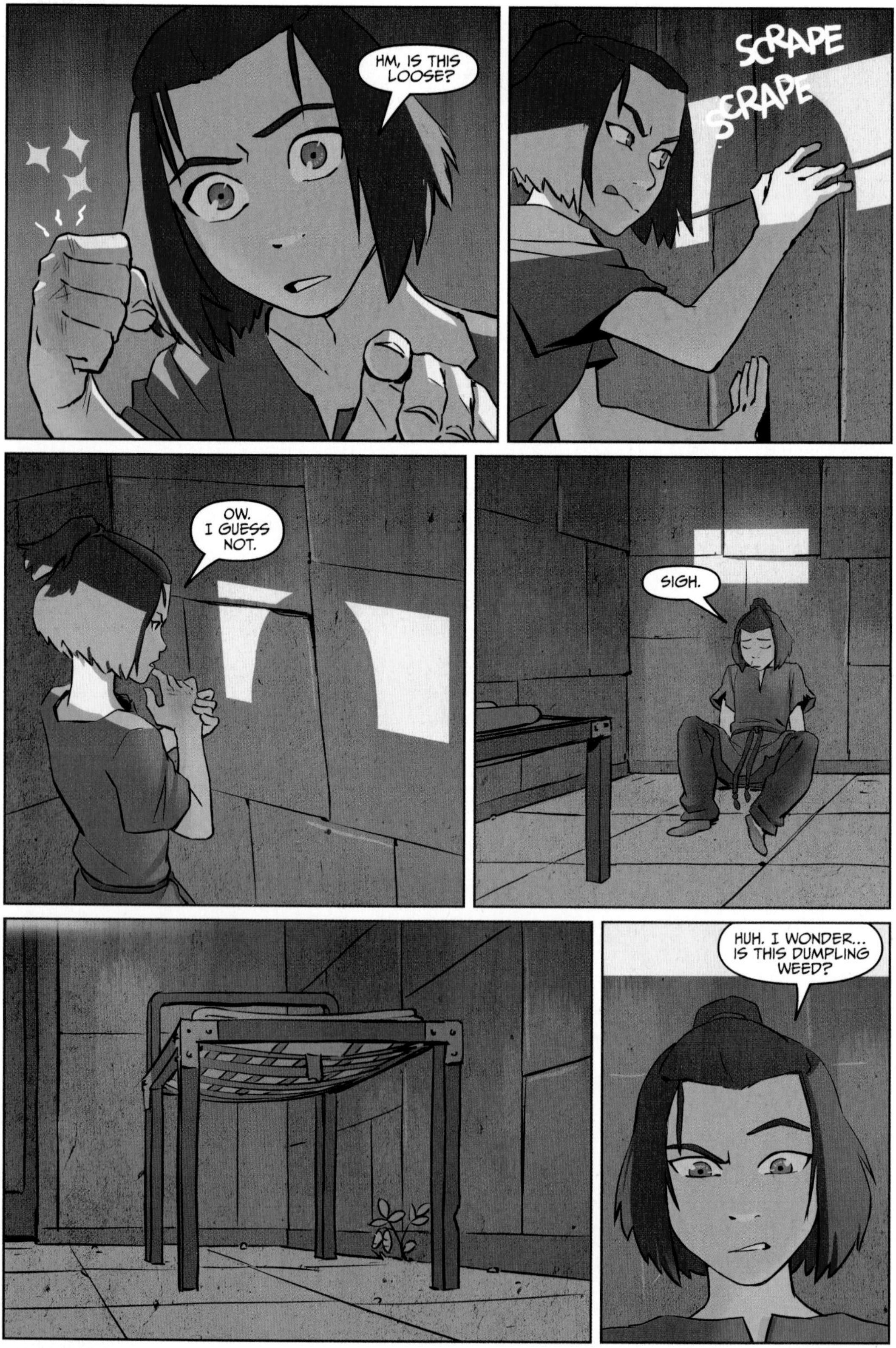
HM, IS THIS LOOSE?
SCRAPE
SCRAPE
OW. I GUESS NOT.
SIGH.
HUH. I WONDER... IS THIS DUMPLING WEED?

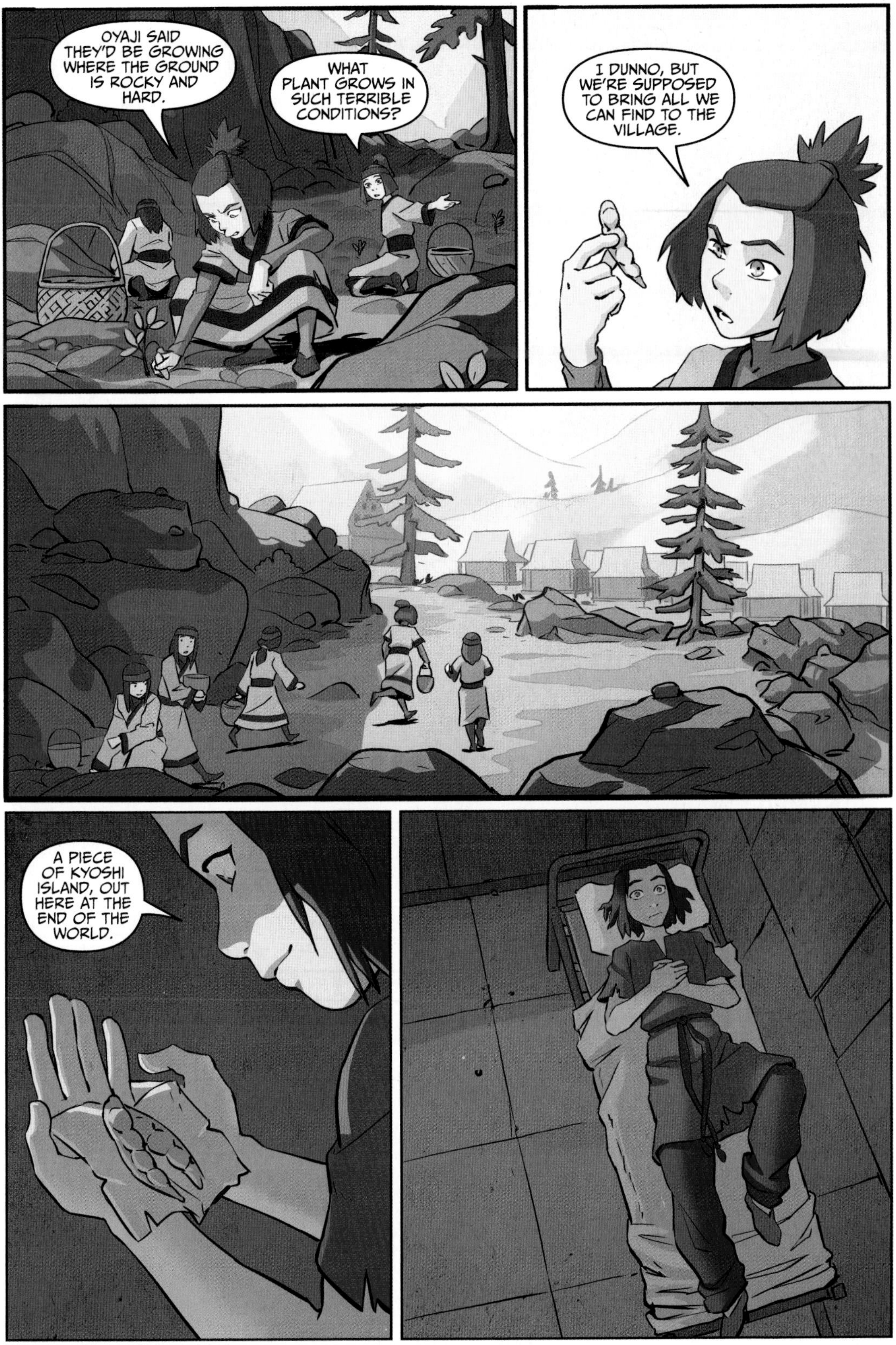
OYAJI SAID THEY'D BE GROWING WHERE THE GROUND IS ROCKY AND HARD.
WHAT PLANT GROWS IN SUCH TERRIBLE CONDITIONS?
I DUNNO, BUT WE'RE SUPPOSED TO BRING ALL WE CAN FIND TO THE VILLAGE.
A PIECE OF KYOSHI ISLAND, OUT HERE AT THE END OF THE WORLD.

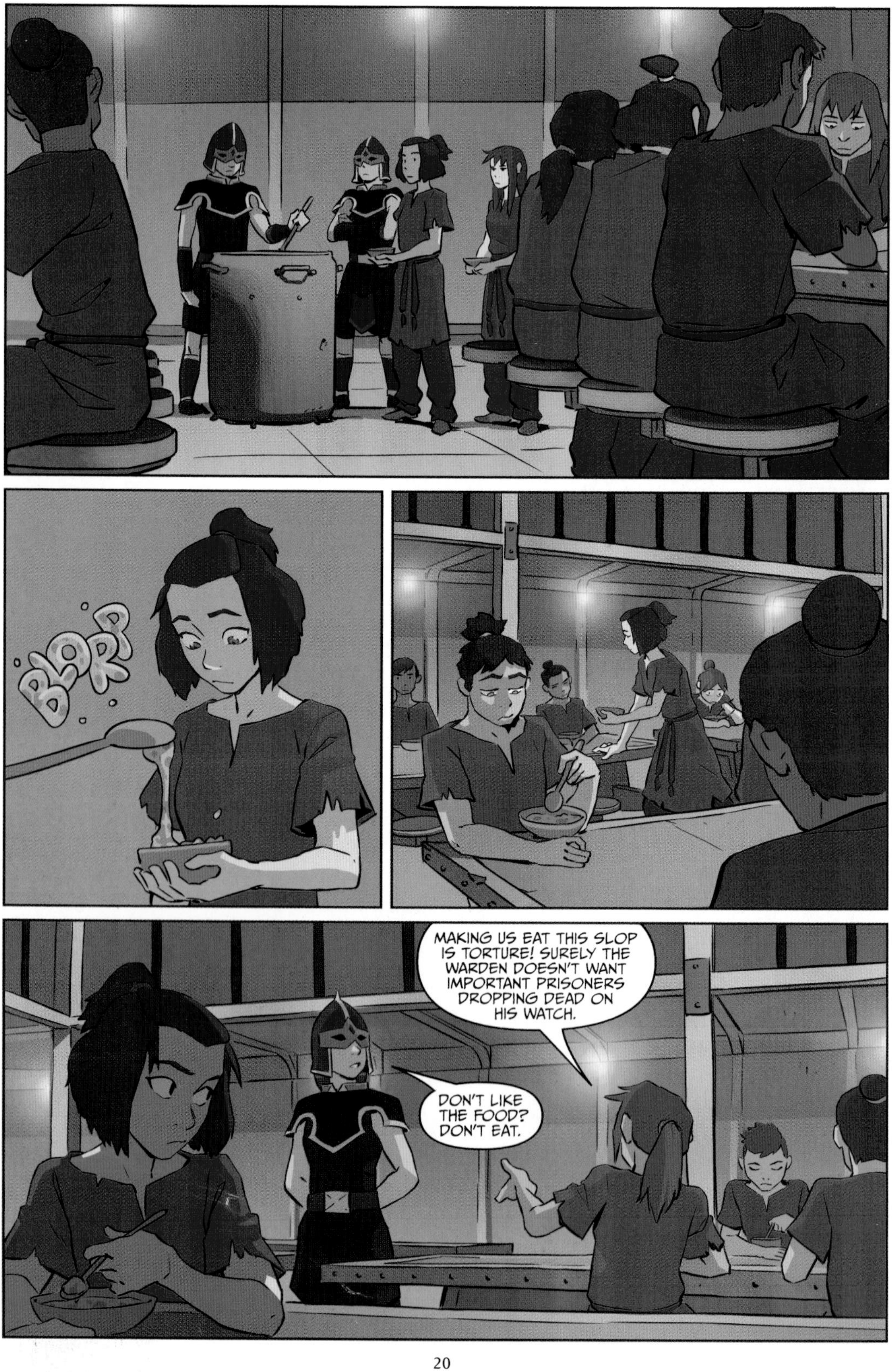
BLORP
MAKING US EAT THIS SLOP IS TORTURE! SURELY THE WARDEN DOESN'T WANT IMPORTANT PRISONERS DROPPING DEAD ON HIS WATCH.
DON'T LIKE THE FOOD? DON'T EAT.

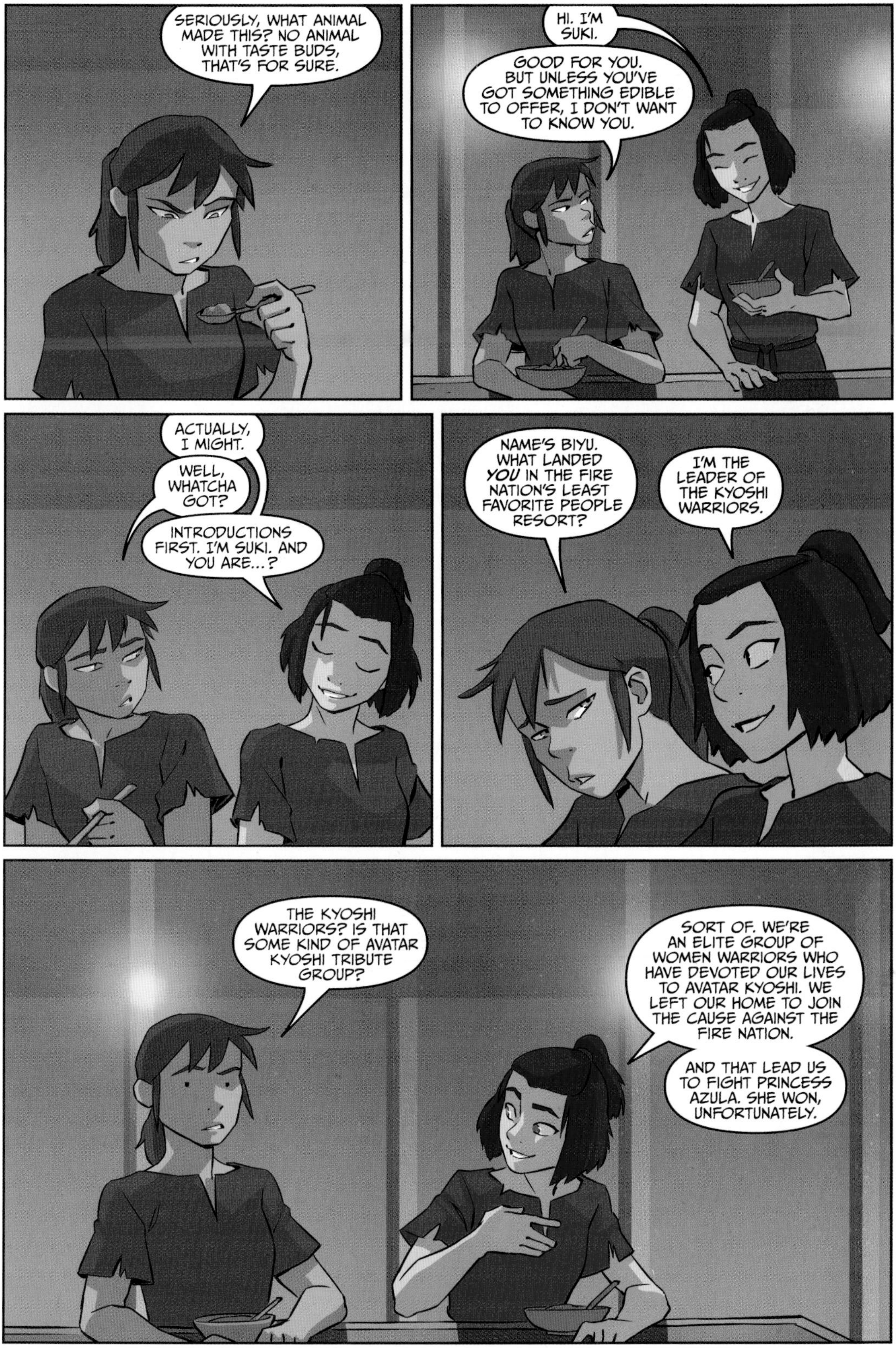
SERIOUSLY, WHAT ANIMAL MADE THIS? NO ANIMAL WITH TASTE BUDS, THAT'S FOR SURE.
HI. I'M SUKI.
GOOD FOR YOU. BUT UNLESS YOU'VE GOT SOMETHING EDIBLE TO OFFER, I DON'T WANT TO KNOW YOU.
ACTUALLY, I MIGHT.
WELL, WHATCHA GOT?
INTRODUCTIONS FIRST. I'M SUKI. AND YOU ARE...?
NAME'S BIYU. WHAT LANDED YOU IN THE FIRE NATION'S LEAST FAVORITE PEOPLE RESORT?
I'M THE LEADER OF THE KYOSHI WARRIORS.
THE KYOSHI WARRIORS? IS THAT SOME KIND OF AVATAR KYOSHI TRIBUTE GROUP?
SORT OF. WE'RE AN ELITE GROUP OF WOMEN WARRIORS WHO HAVE DEVOTED OUR LIVES TO AVATAR KYOSHI. WE LEFT OUR HOME TO JOIN THE CAUSE AGAINST THE FIRE NATION.
AND THAT LEAD US TO FIGHT PRINCESS AZULA. SHE WON, UNFORTUNATELY.

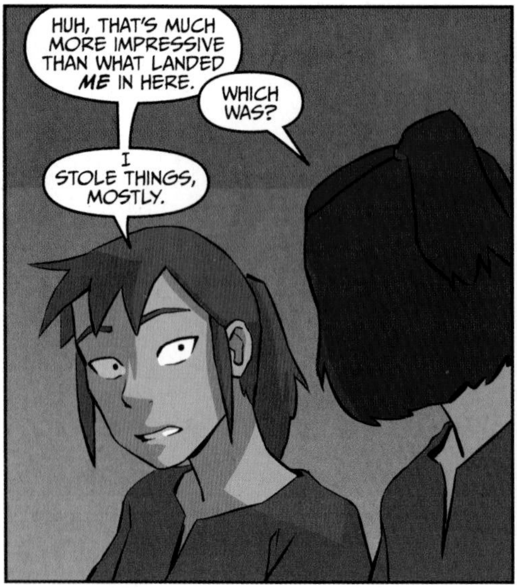
HUH, THAT'S MUCH MORE IMPRESSIVE THAN WHAT LANDED **ME** IN HERE.
WHICH WAS?
I STOLE THINGS, MOSTLY.

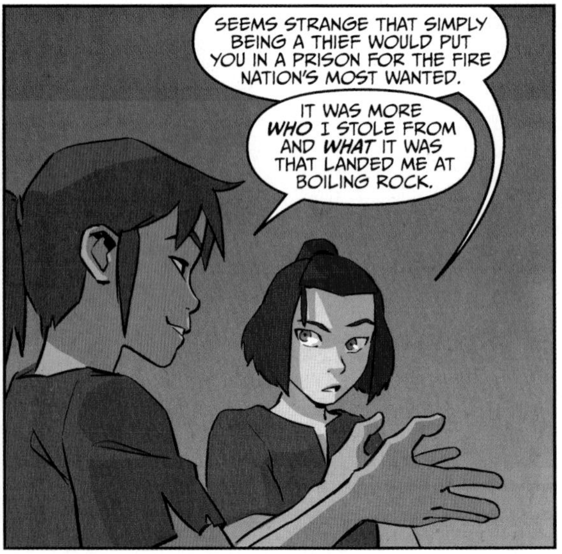
SEEMS STRANGE THAT SIMPLY BEING A THIEF WOULD PUT YOU IN A PRISON FOR THE FIRE NATION'S MOST WANTED.
IT WAS MORE **WHO** I STOLE FROM AND **WHAT** IT WAS THAT LANDED ME AT BOILING ROCK.

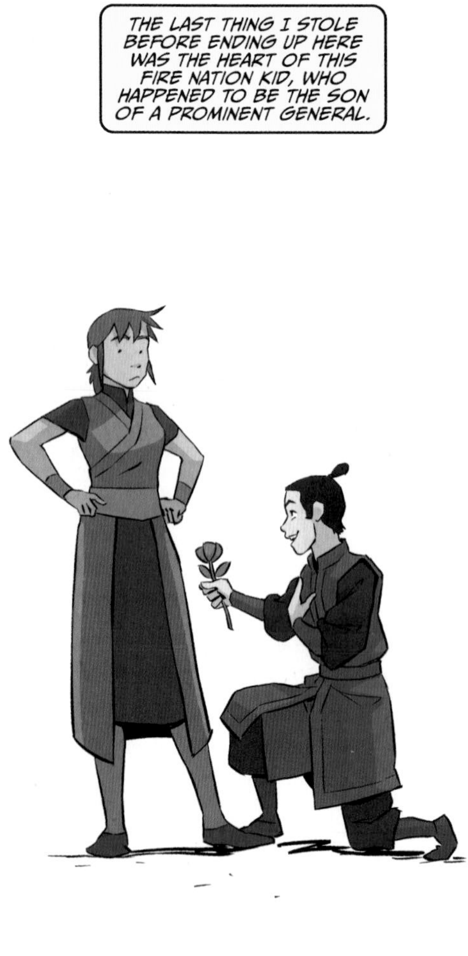
THE LAST THING I STOLE BEFORE ENDING UP HERE WAS THE HEART OF THIS FIRE NATION KID, WHO HAPPENED TO BE THE SON OF A PROMINENT GENERAL.

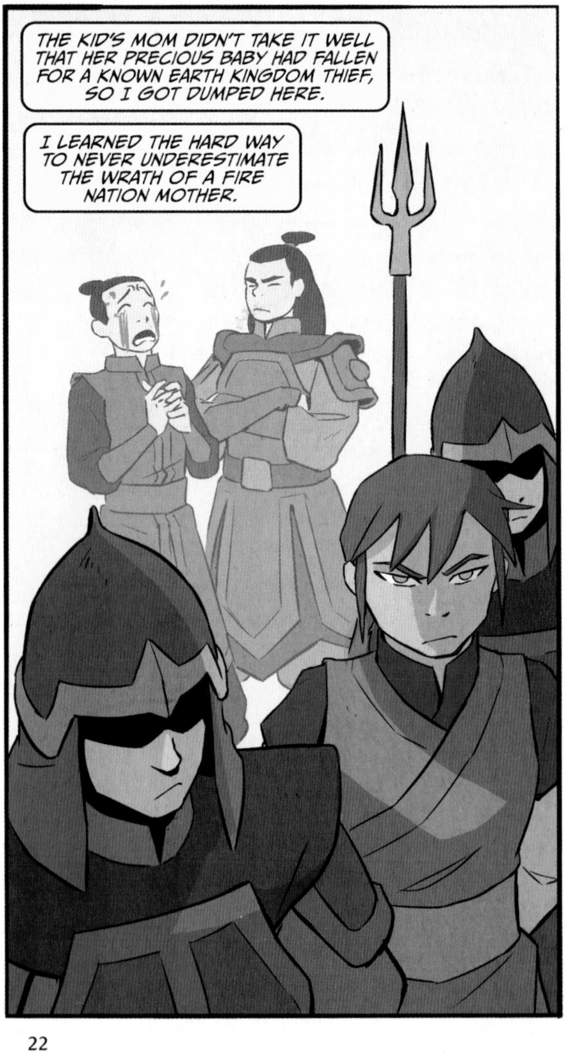
THE KID'S MOM DIDN'T TAKE IT WELL THAT HER PRECIOUS BABY HAD FALLEN FOR A KNOWN EARTH KINGDOM THIEF, SO I GOT DUMPED HERE.
I LEARNED THE HARD WAY TO NEVER UNDERESTIMATE THE WRATH OF A FIRE NATION MOTHER.

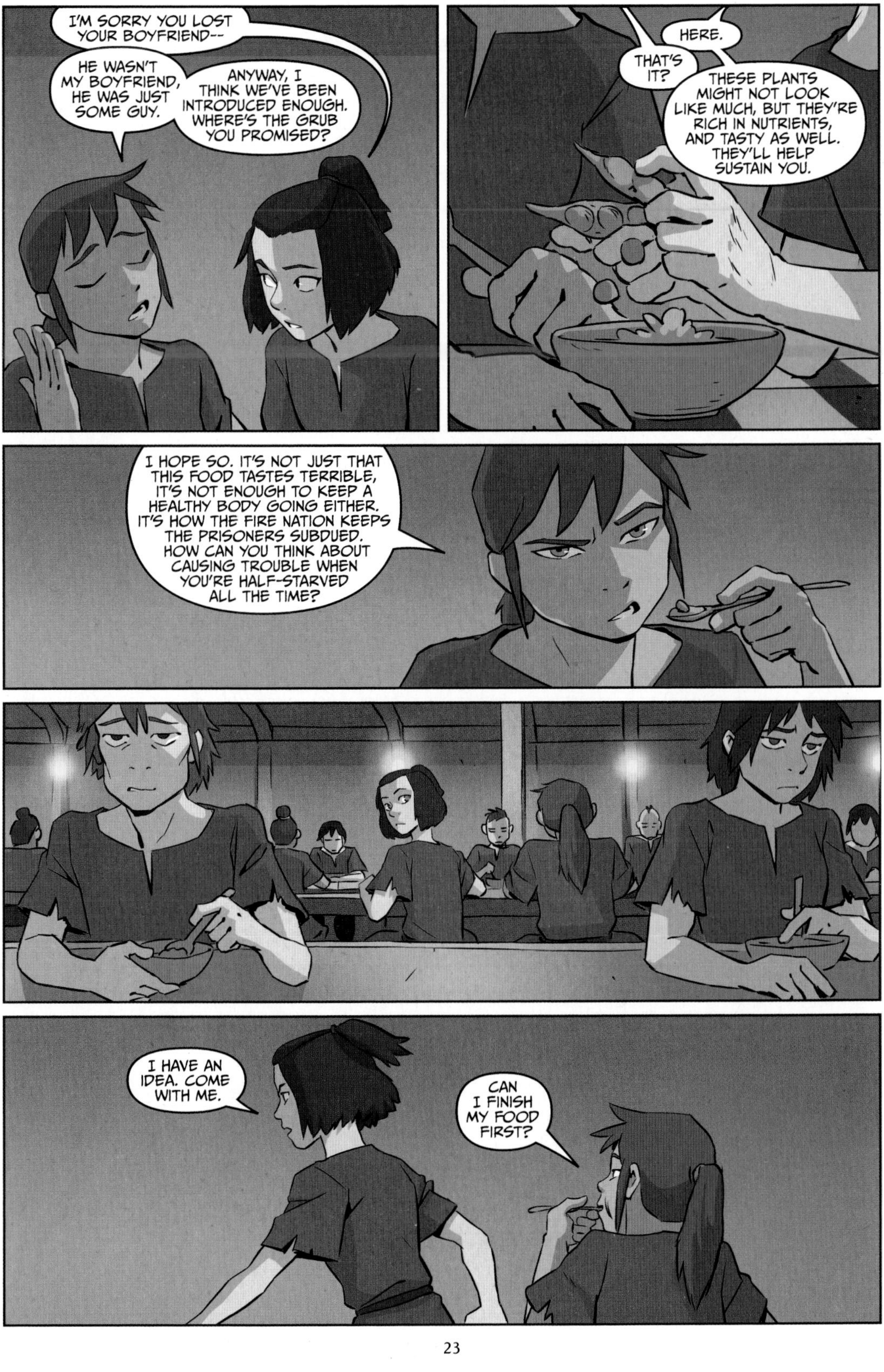
I'M SORRY YOU LOST YOUR BOYFRIEND--
HE WASN'T MY BOYFRIEND, HE WAS JUST SOME GUY.
ANYWAY, I THINK WE'VE BEEN INTRODUCED ENOUGH. WHERE'S THE GRUB YOU PROMISED?
HERE.
THAT'S IT?
THESE PLANTS MIGHT NOT LOOK LIKE MUCH, BUT THEY'RE RICH IN NUTRIENTS, AND TASTY AS WELL. THEY'LL HELP SUSTAIN YOU.
I HOPE SO. IT'S NOT JUST THAT THIS FOOD TASTES TERRIBLE, IT'S NOT ENOUGH TO KEEP A HEALTHY BODY GOING EITHER. IT'S HOW THE FIRE NATION KEEPS THE PRISONERS SUBDUED. HOW CAN YOU THINK ABOUT CAUSING TROUBLE WHEN YOU'RE HALF-STARVED ALL THE TIME?
I HAVE AN IDEA. COME WITH ME.
CAN I FINISH MY FOOD FIRST?

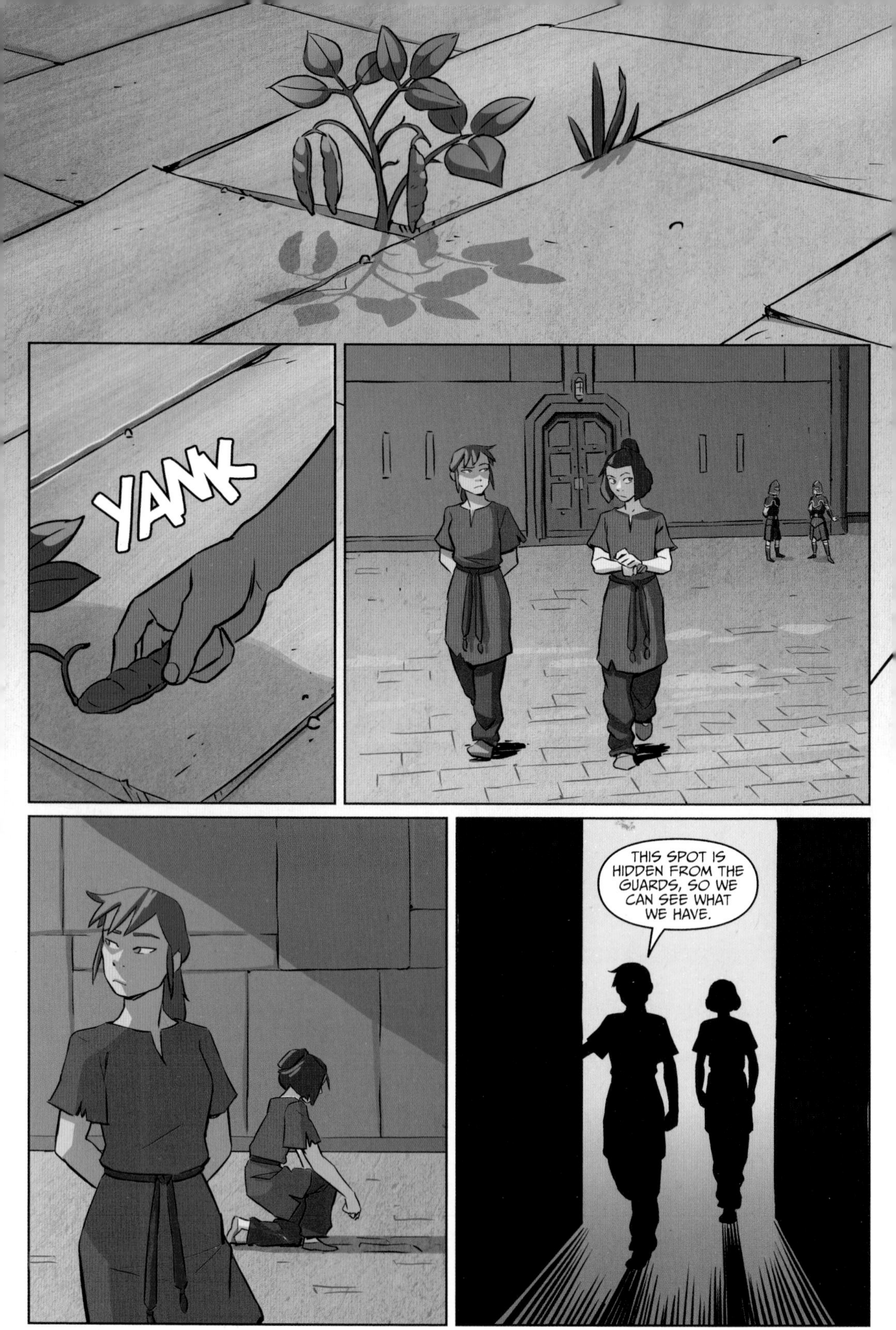
YANK
THIS SPOT IS HIDDEN FROM THE GUARDS, SO WE CAN SEE WHAT WE HAVE.

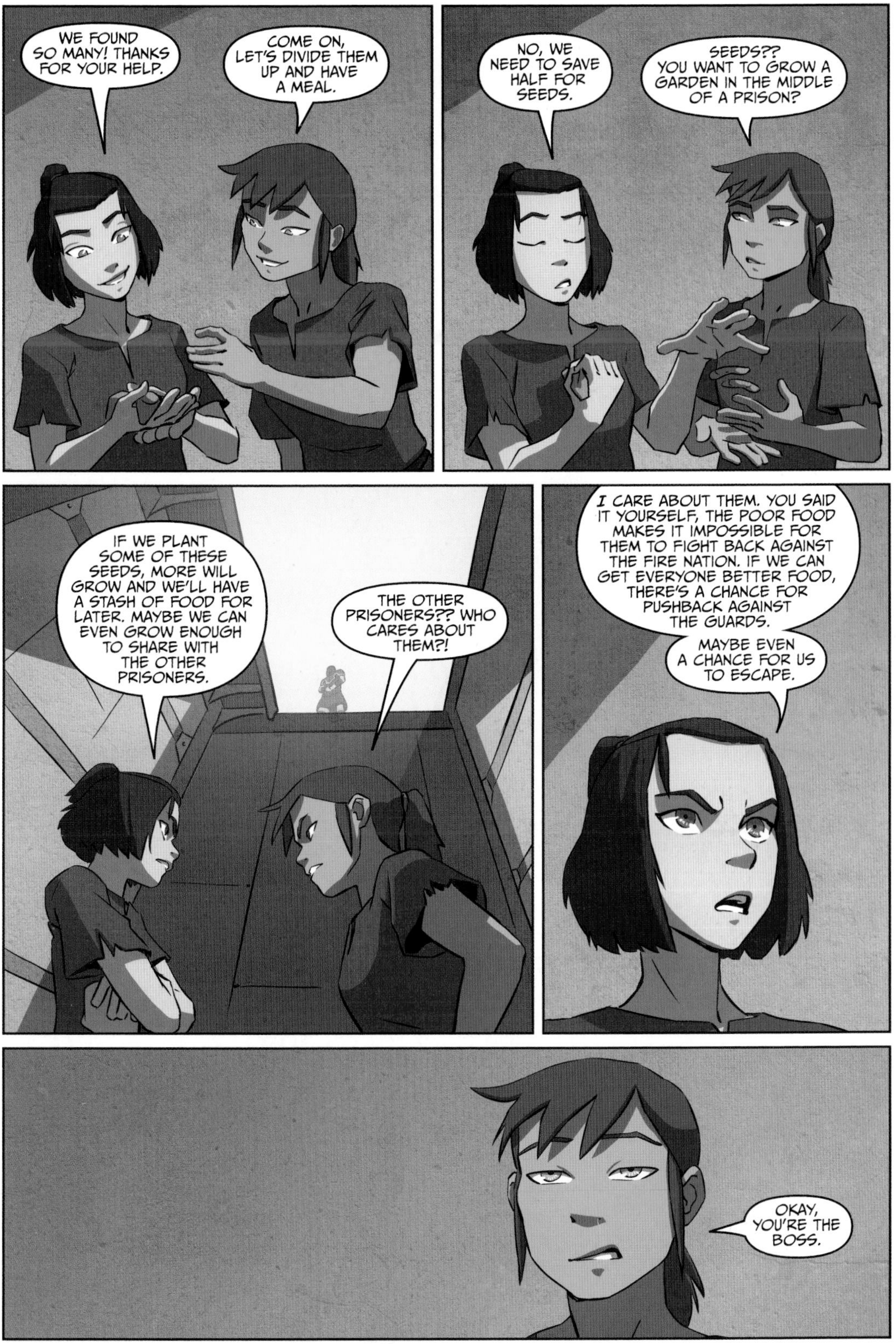
WE FOUND SO MANY! THANKS FOR YOUR HELP.
COME ON, LET'S DIVIDE THEM UP AND HAVE A MEAL.
NO, WE NEED TO SAVE HALF FOR SEEDS.
SEEDS?? YOU WANT TO GROW A GARDEN IN THE MIDDLE OF A PRISON?
IF WE PLANT SOME OF THESE SEEDS, MORE WILL GROW AND WE'LL HAVE A STASH OF FOOD FOR LATER. MAYBE WE CAN EVEN GROW ENOUGH TO SHARE WITH THE OTHER PRISONERS.
THE OTHER PRISONERS?? WHO CARES ABOUT THEM?!
I CARE ABOUT THEM. YOU SAID IT YOURSELF, THE POOR FOOD MAKES IT IMPOSSIBLE FOR THEM TO FIGHT BACK AGAINST THE FIRE NATION. IF WE CAN GET EVERYONE BETTER FOOD, THERE'S A CHANCE FOR PUSHBACK AGAINST THE GUARDS.
MAYBE EVEN A CHANCE FOR US TO ESCAPE.
OKAY, YOU'RE THE BOSS.

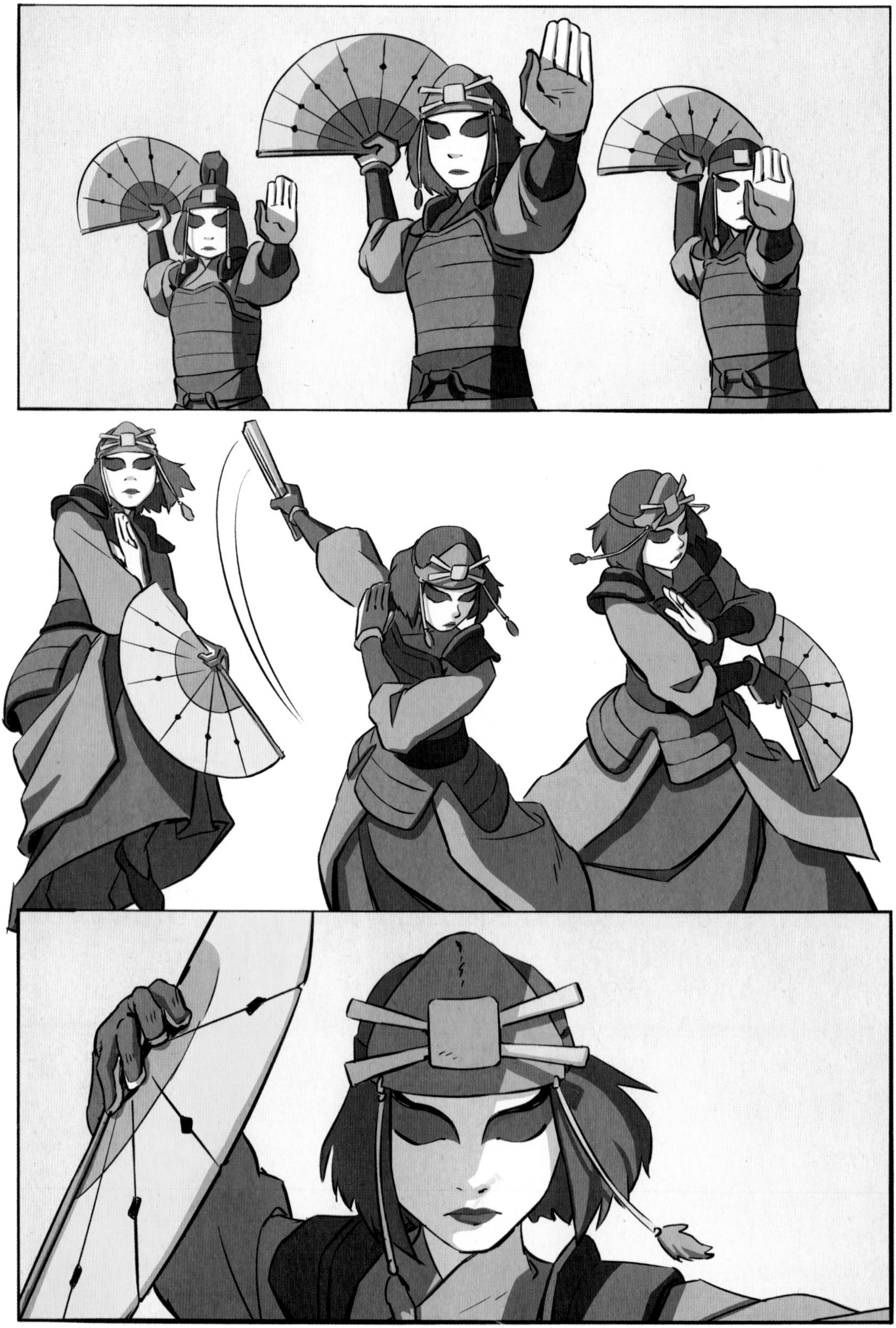

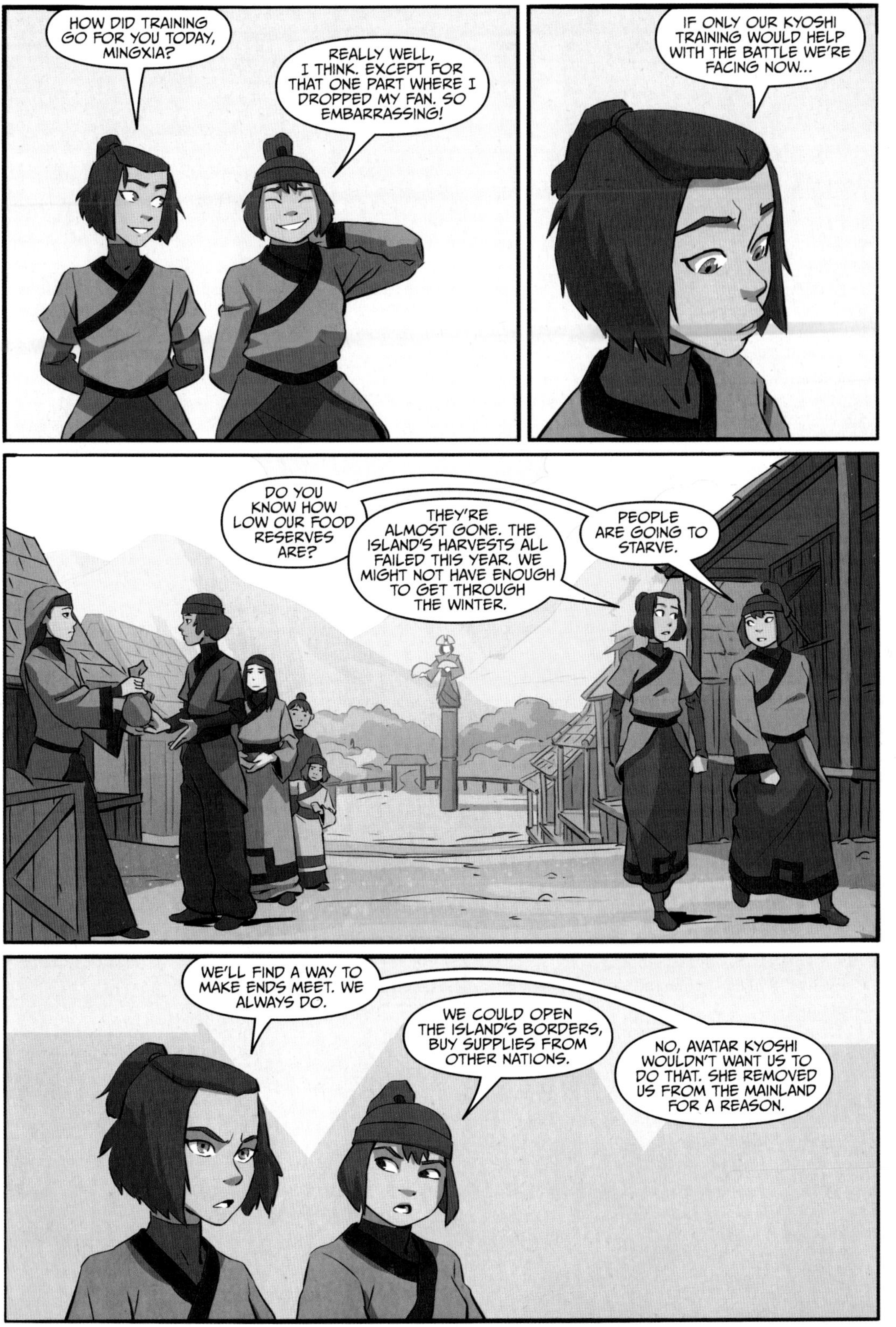
HOW DID TRAINING GO FOR YOU TODAY, MINGXIA?
REALLY WELL, I THINK. EXCEPT FOR THAT ONE PART WHERE I DROPPED MY FAN. SO EMBARRASSING!
IF ONLY OUR KYOSHI TRAINING WOULD HELP WITH THE BATTLE WE'RE FACING NOW...
DO YOU KNOW HOW LOW OUR FOOD RESERVES ARE?
THEY'RE ALMOST GONE. THE ISLAND'S HARVESTS ALL FAILED THIS YEAR. WE MIGHT NOT HAVE ENOUGH TO GET THROUGH THE WINTER.
PEOPLE ARE GOING TO STARVE.
WE'LL FIND A WAY TO MAKE ENDS MEET. WE ALWAYS DO.
WE COULD OPEN THE ISLAND'S BORDERS, BUY SUPPLIES FROM OTHER NATIONS.
NO, AVATAR KYOSHI WOULDN'T WANT US TO DO THAT. SHE REMOVED US FROM THE MAINLAND FOR A REASON.

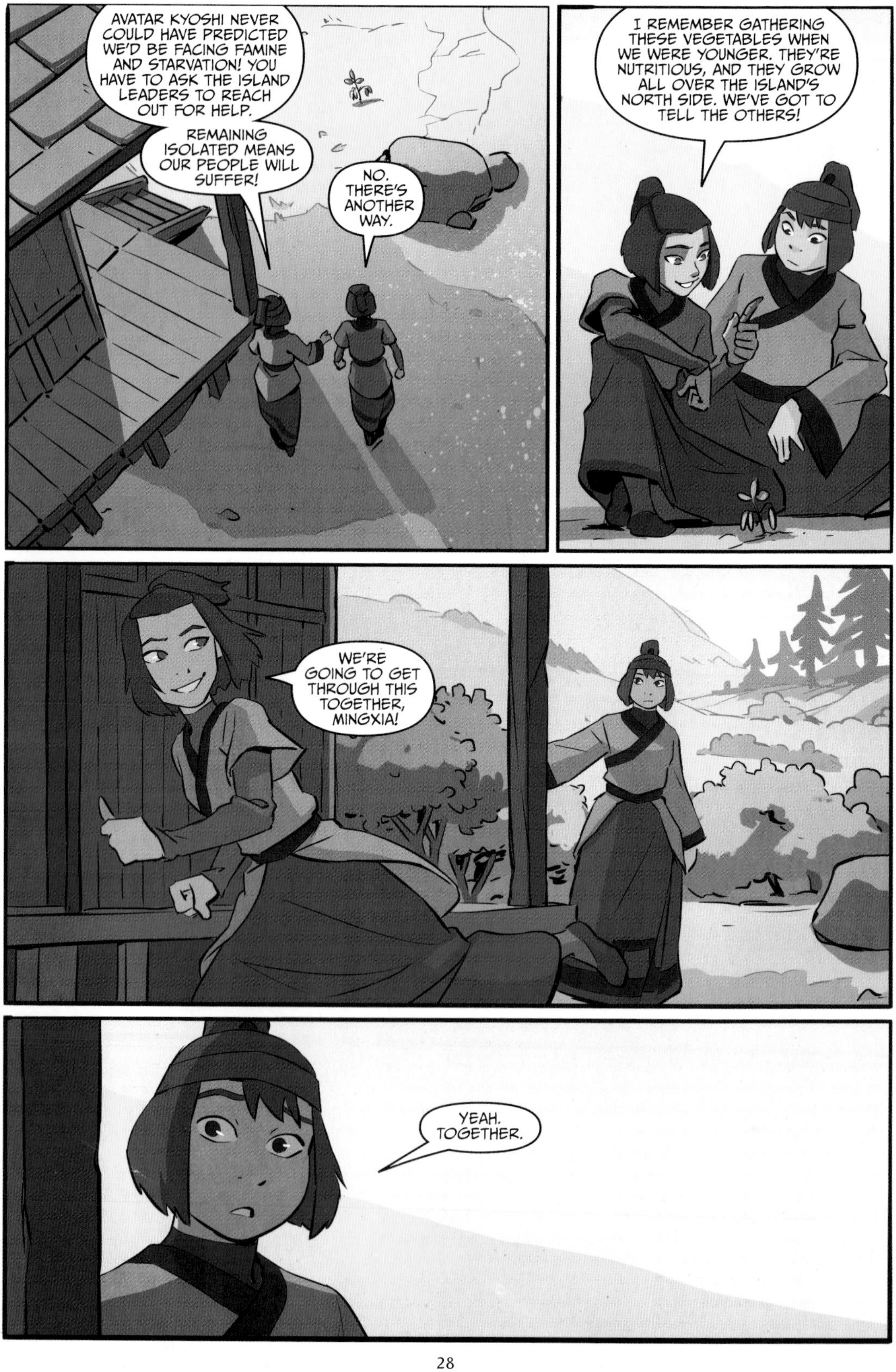
AVATAR KYOSHI NEVER COULD HAVE PREDICTED WE'D BE FACING FAMINE AND STARVATION! YOU HAVE TO ASK THE ISLAND LEADERS TO REACH OUT FOR HELP.
REMAINING ISOLATED MEANS OUR PEOPLE WILL SUFFER!
NO. THERE'S ANOTHER WAY.
I REMEMBER GATHERING THESE VEGETABLES WHEN WE WERE YOUNGER. THEY'RE NUTRITIOUS, AND THEY GROW ALL OVER THE ISLAND'S NORTH SIDE. WE'VE GOT TO TELL THE OTHERS!
WE'RE GOING TO GET THROUGH THIS TOGETHER, MINGXIA!
YEAH. TOGETHER.

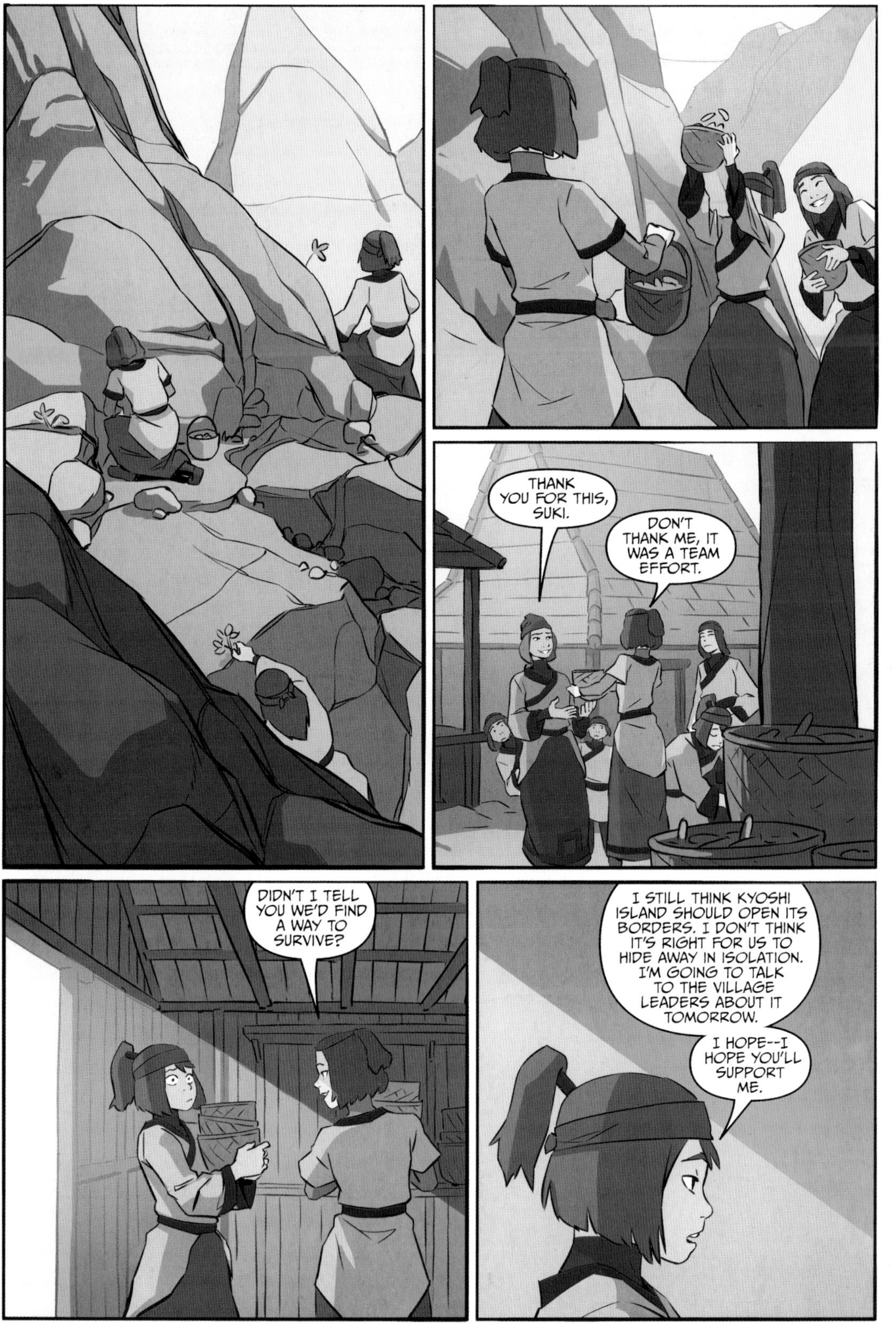
THANK YOU FOR THIS, SUKI.
DON'T THANK ME, IT WAS A TEAM EFFORT.
DIDN'T I TELL YOU WE'D FIND A WAY TO SURVIVE?
I STILL THINK KYOSHI ISLAND SHOULD OPEN ITS BORDERS. I DON'T THINK IT'S RIGHT FOR US TO HIDE AWAY IN ISOLATION. I'M GOING TO TALK TO THE VILLAGE LEADERS ABOUT IT TOMORROW.
I HOPE--I HOPE YOU'LL SUPPORT ME.

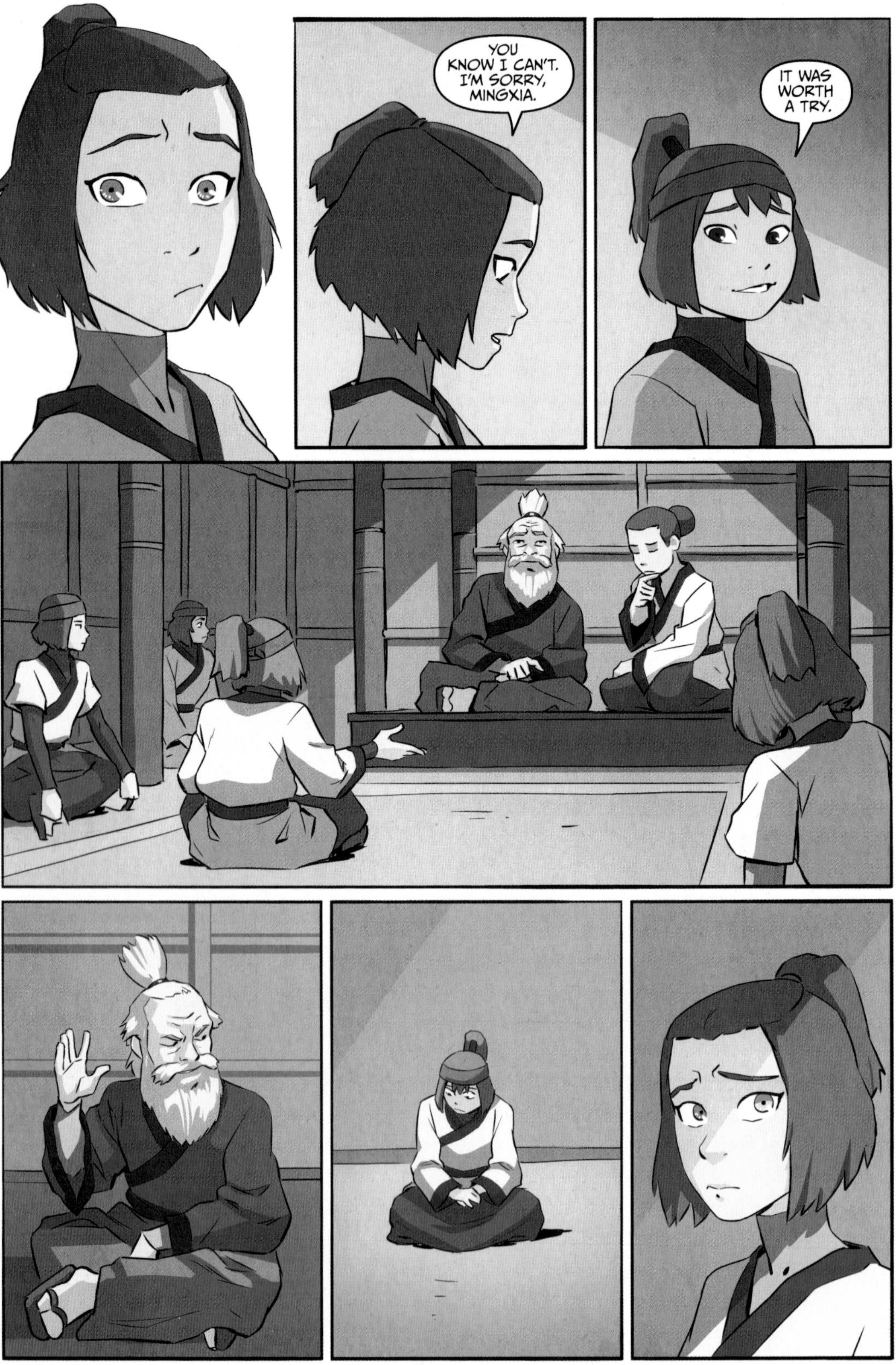
YOU KNOW I CAN'T. I'M SORRY, MINGXIA.
IT WAS WORTH A TRY.

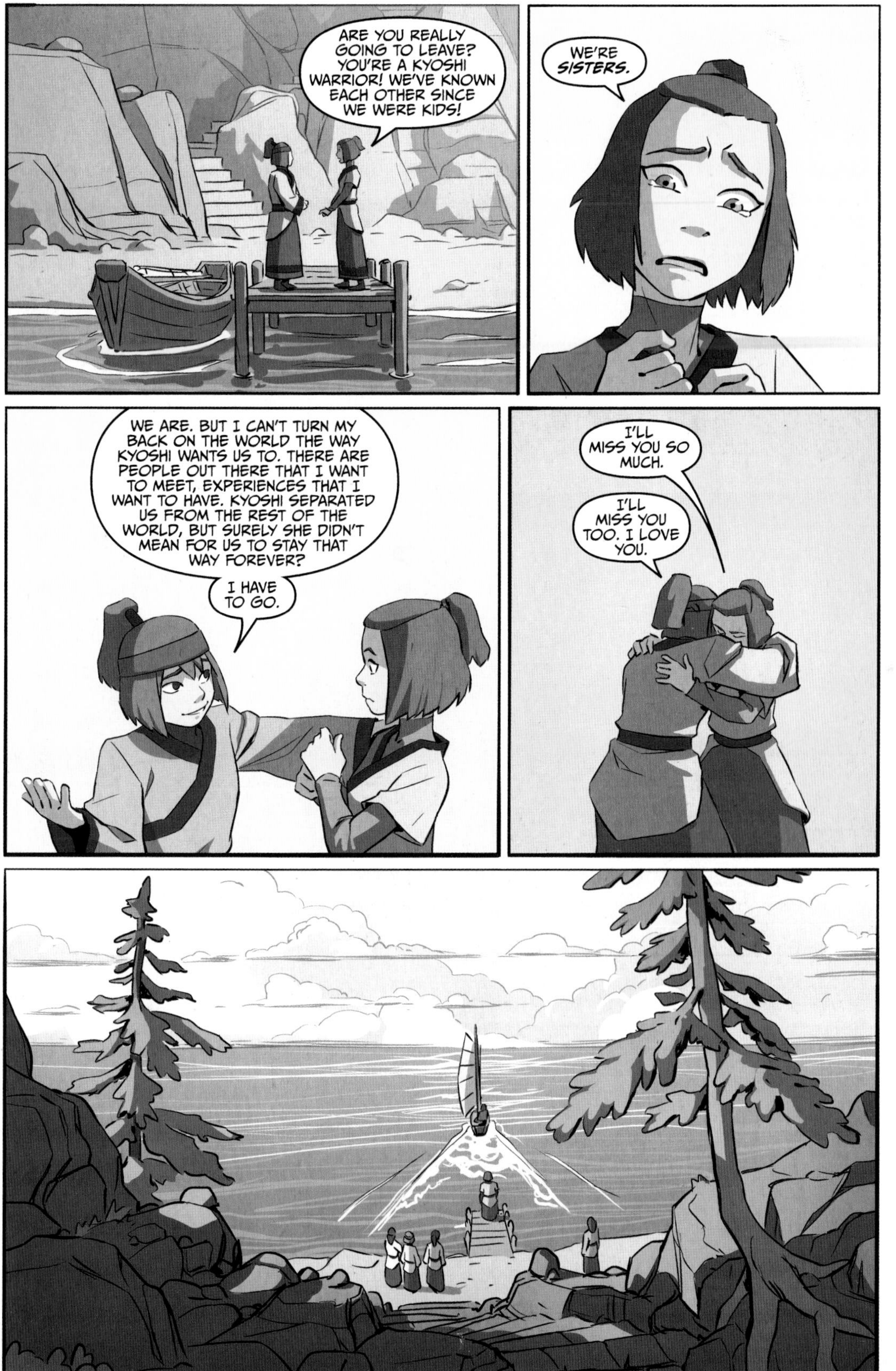
ARE YOU REALLY GOING TO LEAVE? YOU'RE A KYOSHI WARRIOR! WE'VE KNOWN EACH OTHER SINCE WE WERE KIDS!
WE'RE SISTERS.
WE ARE. BUT I CAN'T TURN MY BACK ON THE WORLD THE WAY KYOSHI WANTS US TO. THERE ARE PEOPLE OUT THERE THAT I WANT TO MEET, EXPERIENCES THAT I WANT TO HAVE. KYOSHI SEPARATED US FROM THE REST OF THE WORLD, BUT SURELY SHE DIDN'T MEAN FOR US TO STAY THAT WAY FOREVER?
I HAVE TO GO.
I'LL MISS YOU SO MUCH.
I'LL MISS YOU TOO. I LOVE YOU.

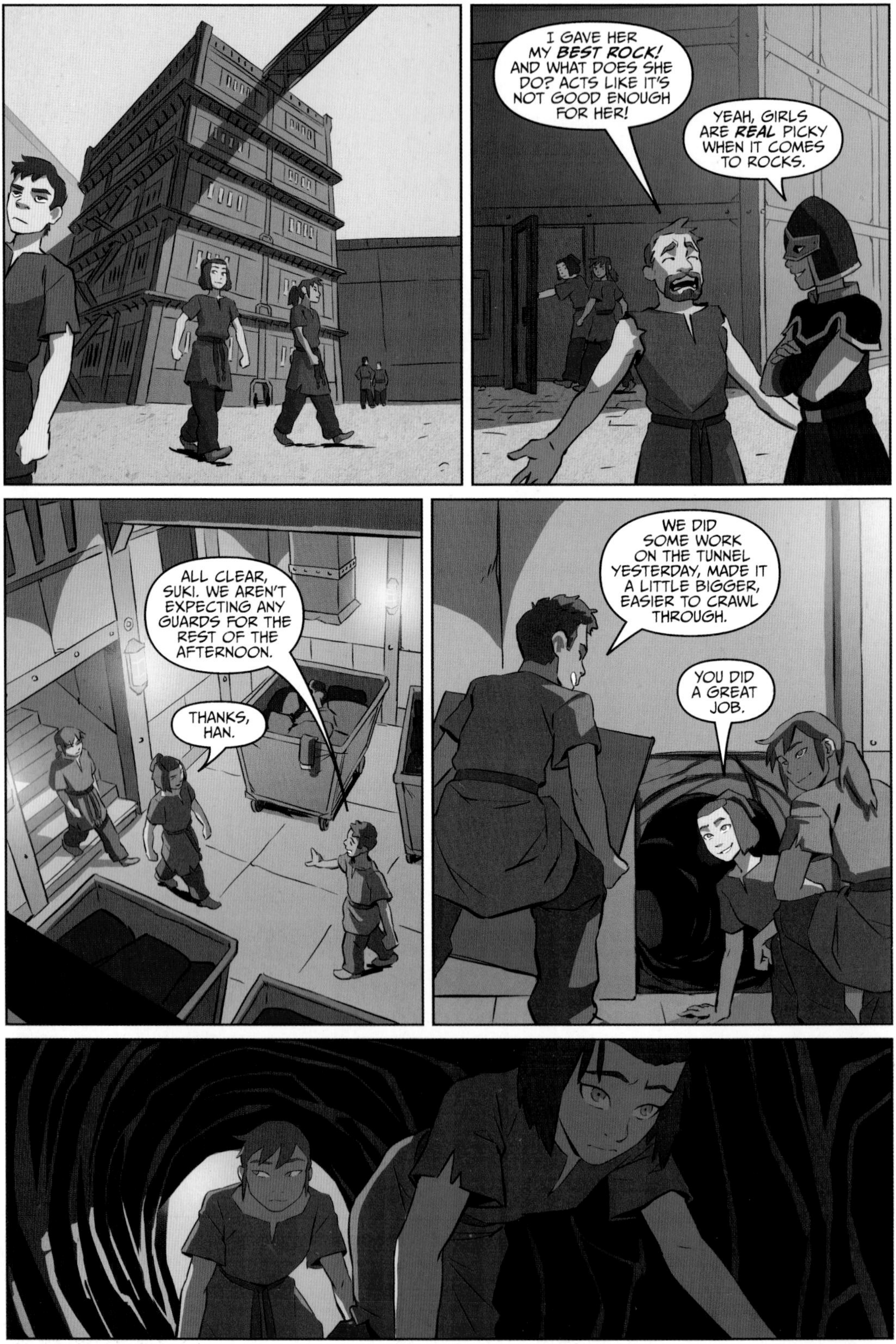
I GAVE HER MY BEST ROCK! AND WHAT DOES SHE DO? ACTS LIKE IT'S NOT GOOD ENOUGH FOR HER!
YEAH, GIRLS ARE REAL PICKY WHEN IT COMES TO ROCKS.
ALL CLEAR, SUKI. WE AREN'T EXPECTING ANY GUARDS FOR THE REST OF THE AFTERNOON.
THANKS, HAN.
WE DID SOME WORK ON THE TUNNEL YESTERDAY, MADE IT A LITTLE BIGGER, EASIER TO CRAWL THROUGH.
YOU DID A GREAT JOB.

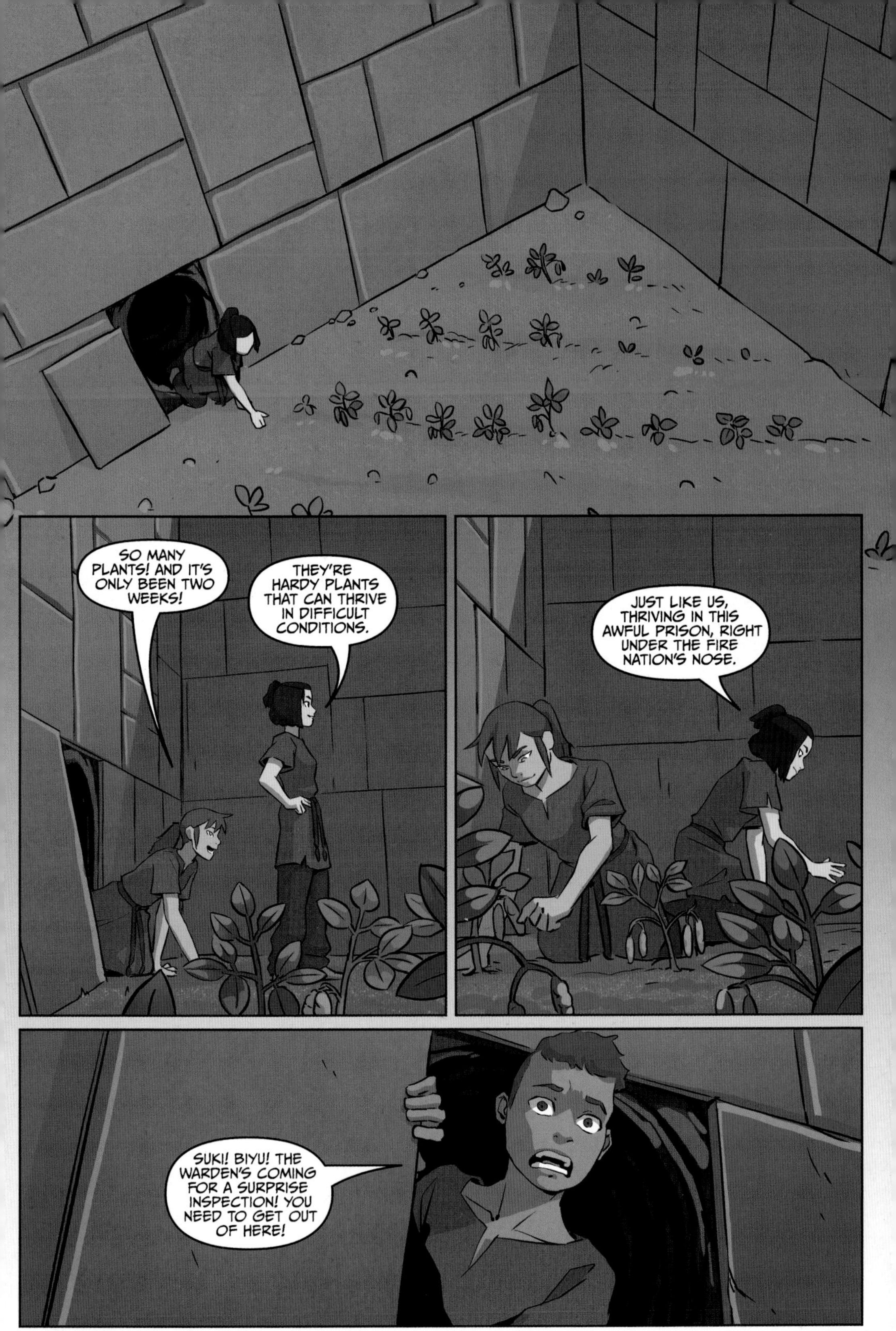
SO MANY PLANTS! AND IT'S ONLY BEEN TWO WEEKS!
THEY'RE HARDY PLANTS THAT CAN THRIVE IN DIFFICULT CONDITIONS.
JUST LIKE US, THRIVING IN THIS AWFUL PRISON, RIGHT UNDER THE FIRE NATION'S NOSE.
SUKI! BIYU! THE WARDEN'S COMING FOR A SURPRISE INSPECTION! YOU NEED TO GET OUT OF HERE!

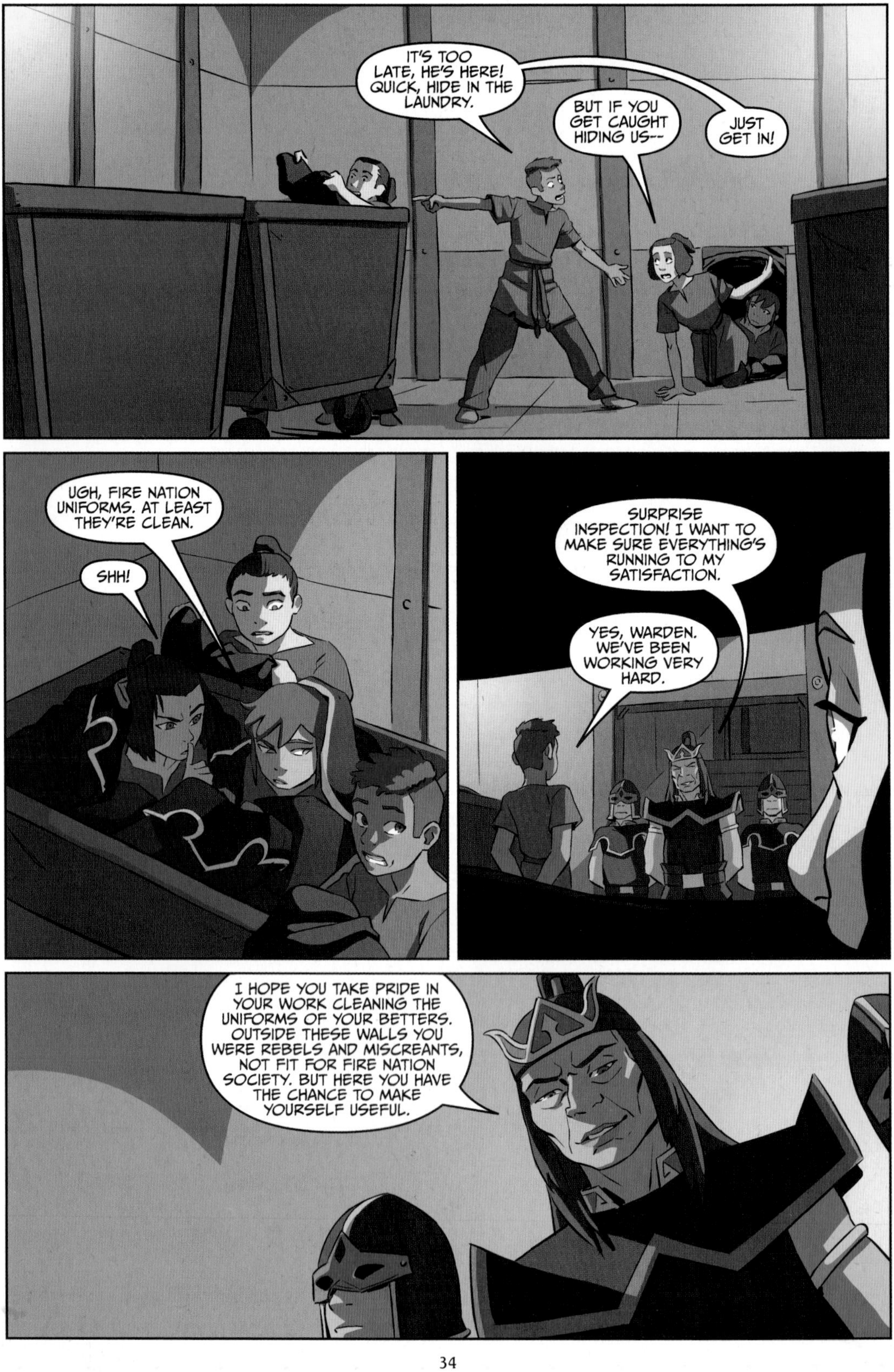
IT'S TOO LATE, HE'S HERE! QUICK, HIDE IN THE LAUNDRY.
BUT IF YOU GET CAUGHT HIDING US--
JUST GET IN!
UGH, FIRE NATION UNIFORMS. AT LEAST THEY'RE CLEAN.
SHH!
SURPRISE INSPECTION! I WANT TO MAKE SURE EVERYTHING'S RUNNING TO MY SATISFACTION.
YES, WARDEN. WE'VE BEEN WORKING VERY HARD.
I HOPE YOU TAKE PRIDE IN YOUR WORK CLEANING THE UNIFORMS OF YOUR BETTERS. OUTSIDE THESE WALLS YOU WERE REBELS AND MISCREANTS, NOT FIT FOR FIRE NATION SOCIETY. BUT HERE YOU HAVE THE CHANCE TO MAKE YOURSELF USEFUL.

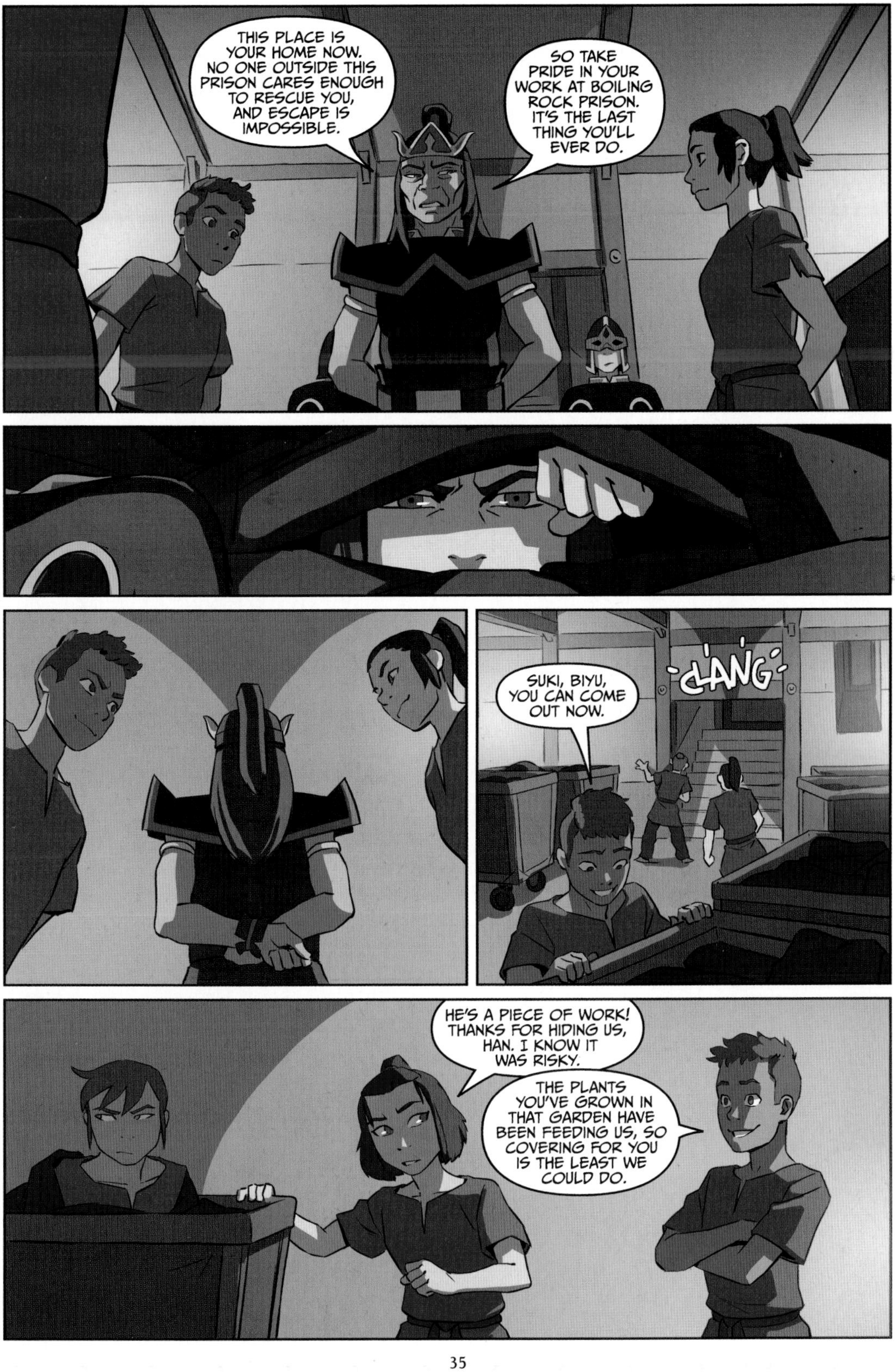
THIS PLACE IS YOUR HOME NOW. NO ONE OUTSIDE THIS PRISON CARES ENOUGH TO RESCUE YOU, AND ESCAPE IS IMPOSSIBLE.
SO TAKE PRIDE IN YOUR WORK AT BOILING ROCK PRISON. IT'S THE LAST THING YOU'LL EVER DO.
SUKI, BIYU, YOU CAN COME OUT NOW.
CLANG
HE'S A PIECE OF WORK! THANKS FOR HIDING US, HAN. I KNOW IT WAS RISKY.
THE PLANTS YOU'VE GROWN IN THAT GARDEN HAVE BEEN FEEDING US, SO COVERING FOR YOU IS THE LEAST WE COULD DO.

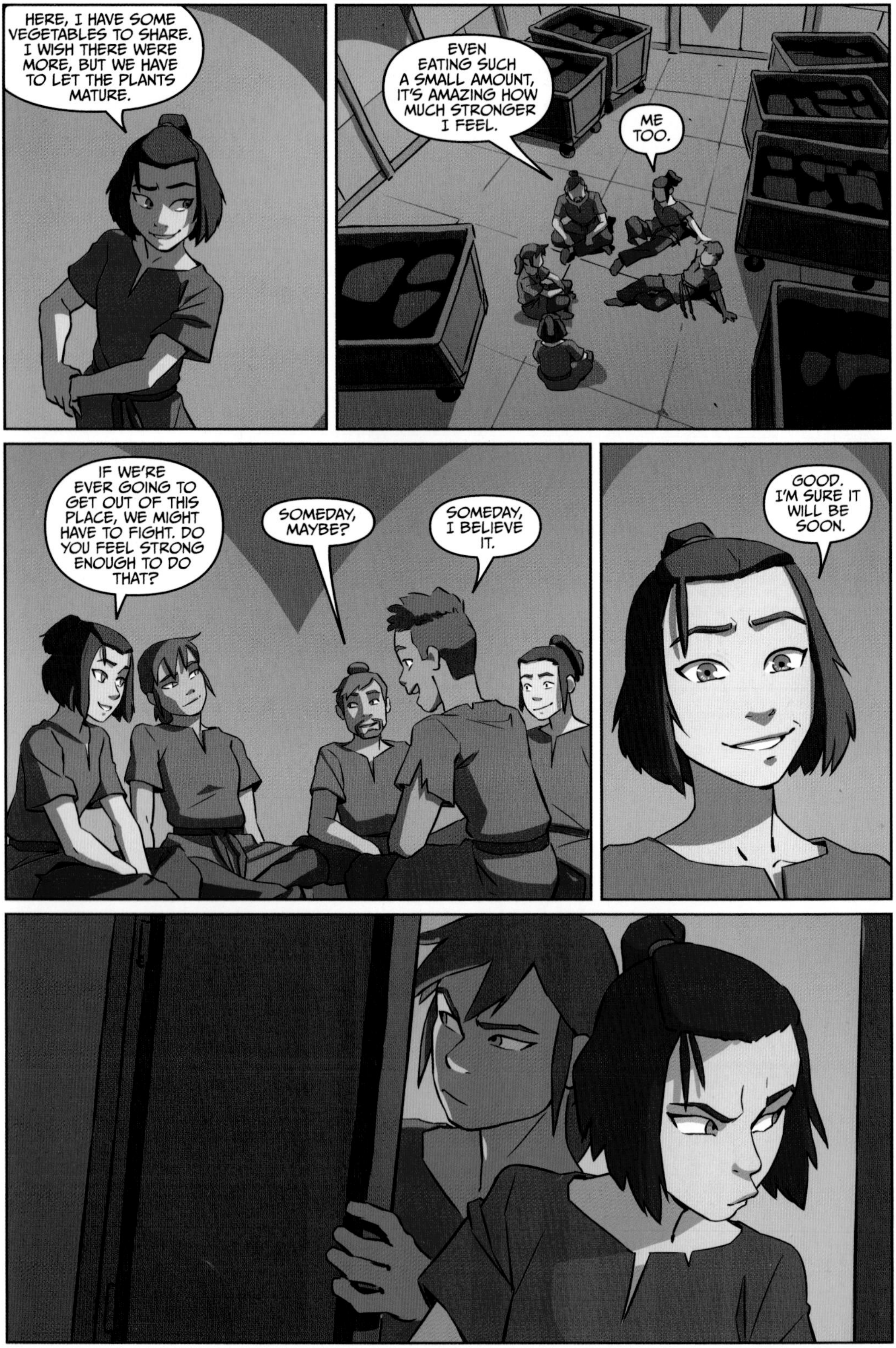
HERE, I HAVE SOME VEGETABLES TO SHARE. I WISH THERE WERE MORE, BUT WE HAVE TO LET THE PLANTS MATURE.
EVEN EATING SUCH A SMALL AMOUNT, IT'S AMAZING HOW MUCH STRONGER I FEEL.
ME TOO.
IF WE'RE EVER GOING TO GET OUT OF THIS PLACE, WE MIGHT HAVE TO FIGHT. DO YOU FEEL STRONG ENOUGH TO DO THAT?
SOMEDAY, MAYBE?
SOMEDAY, I BELIEVE IT.
GOOD. I'M SURE IT WILL BE SOON.

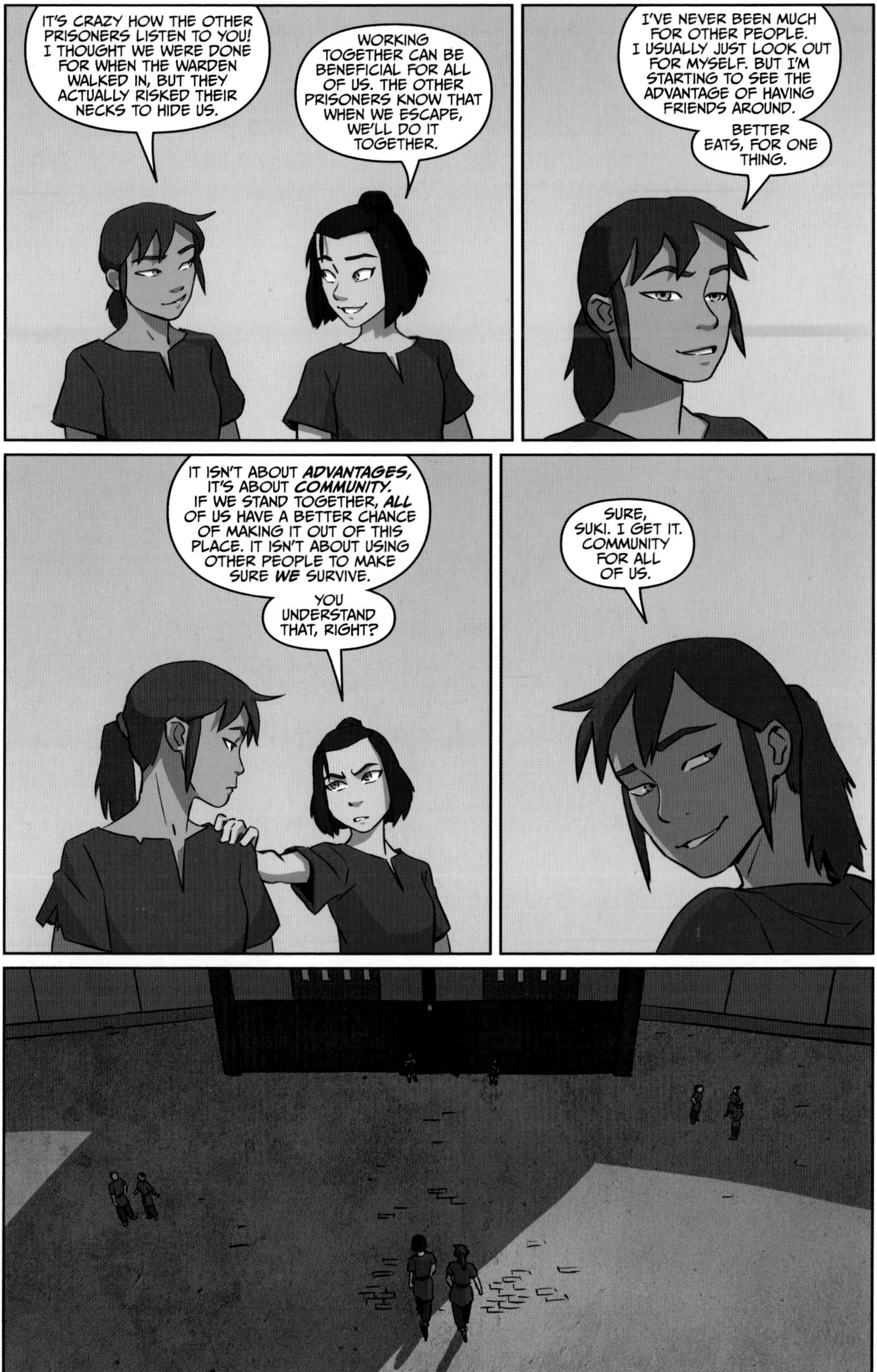
IT'S CRAZY HOW THE OTHER PRISONERS LISTEN TO YOU! I THOUGHT WE WERE DONE FOR WHEN THE WARDEN WALKED IN, BUT THEY ACTUALLY RISKED THEIR NECKS TO HIDE US.
WORKING TOGETHER CAN BE BENEFICIAL FOR ALL OF US. THE OTHER PRISONERS KNOW THAT WHEN WE ESCAPE, WE'LL DO IT TOGETHER.
I'VE NEVER BEEN MUCH FOR OTHER PEOPLE. I USUALLY JUST LOOK OUT FOR MYSELF. BUT I'M STARTING TO SEE THE ADVANTAGE OF HAVING FRIENDS AROUND.
BETTER EATS, FOR ONE THING.
IT ISN'T ABOUT ***ADVANTAGES,*** IT'S ABOUT ***COMMUNITY.*** IF WE STAND TOGETHER, ***ALL*** OF US HAVE A BETTER CHANCE OF MAKING IT OUT OF THIS PLACE. IT ISN'T ABOUT USING OTHER PEOPLE TO MAKE SURE ***WE*** SURVIVE.
YOU UNDERSTAND THAT, RIGHT?
SURE, SUKI. I GET IT. COMMUNITY FOR ALL OF US.

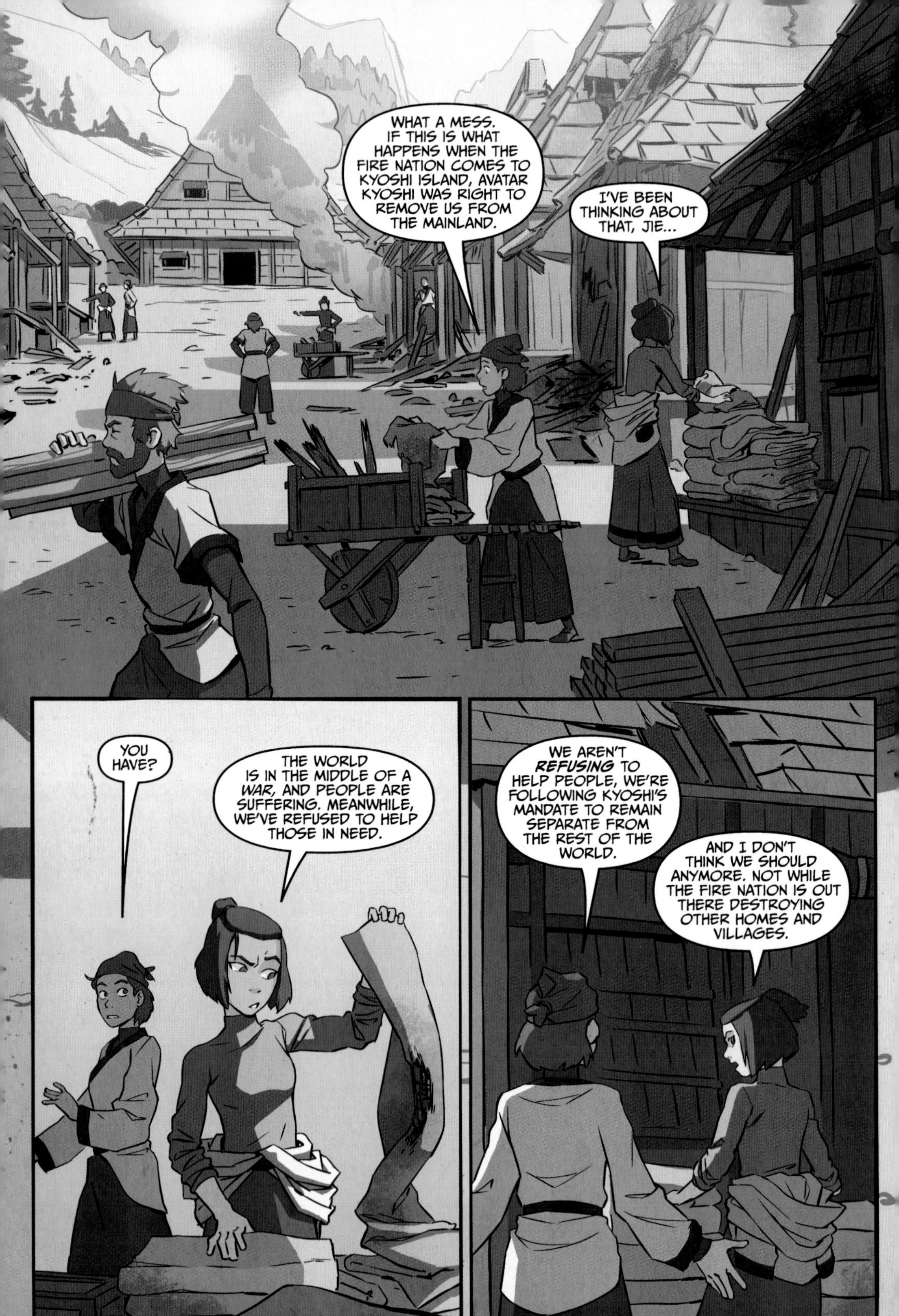
WHAT A MESS. IF THIS IS WHAT HAPPENS WHEN THE FIRE NATION COMES TO KYOSHI ISLAND, AVATAR KYOSHI WAS RIGHT TO REMOVE US FROM THE MAINLAND.
I'VE BEEN THINKING ABOUT THAT, JIE...
YOU HAVE?
THE WORLD IS IN THE MIDDLE OF A *WAR*, AND PEOPLE ARE SUFFERING. MEANWHILE, WE'VE REFUSED TO HELP THOSE IN NEED.
WE AREN'T ***REFUSING*** TO HELP PEOPLE, WE'RE FOLLOWING KYOSHI'S MANDATE TO REMAIN SEPARATE FROM THE REST OF THE WORLD.
AND I DON'T THINK WE SHOULD ANYMORE. NOT WHILE THE FIRE NATION IS OUT THERE DESTROYING OTHER HOMES AND VILLAGES.

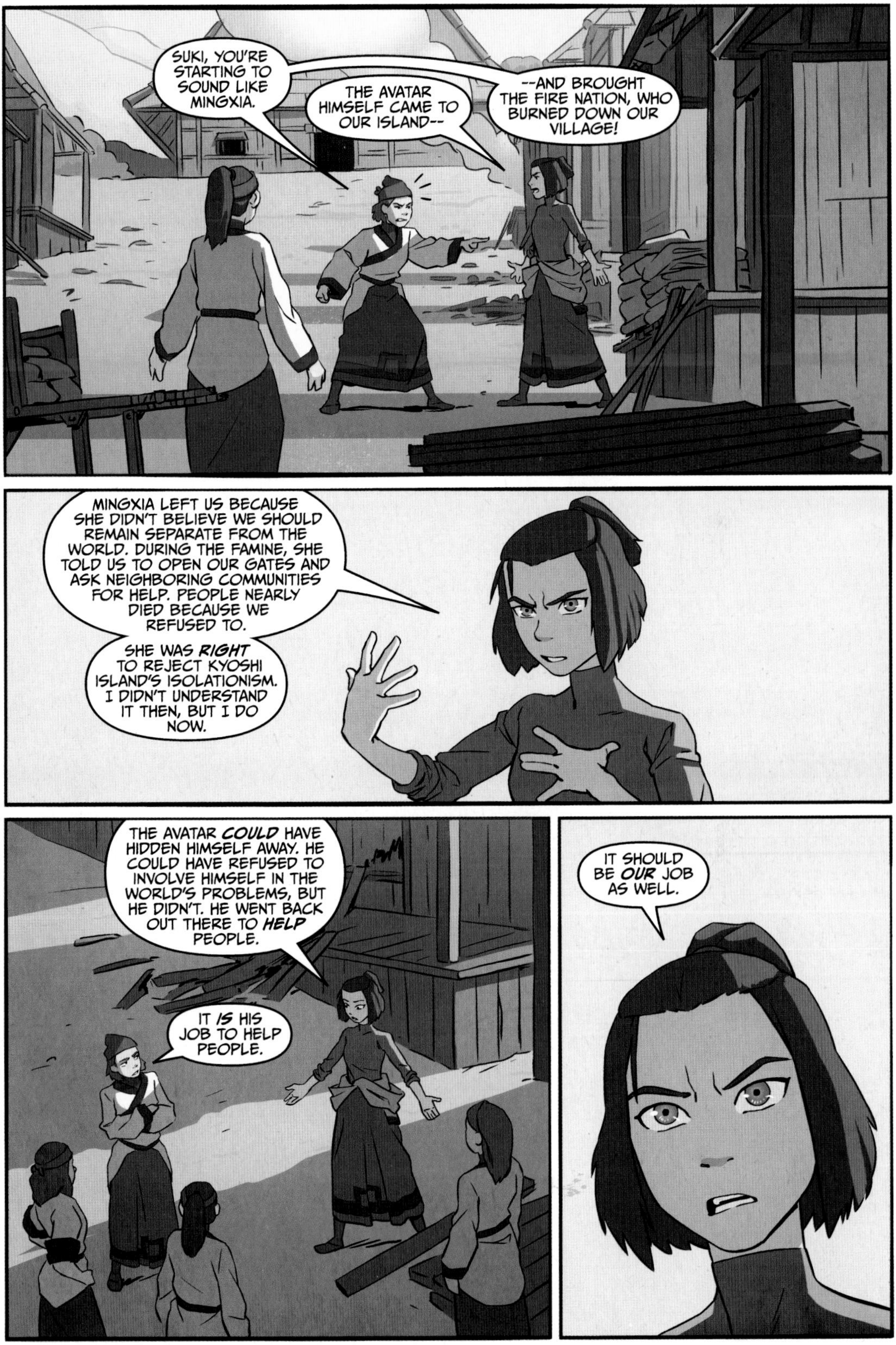
SUKI, YOU'RE STARTING TO SOUND LIKE MINGXIA.
THE AVATAR HIMSELF CAME TO OUR ISLAND--
--AND BROUGHT THE FIRE NATION, WHO BURNED DOWN OUR VILLAGE!
MINGXIA LEFT US BECAUSE SHE DIDN'T BELIEVE WE SHOULD REMAIN SEPARATE FROM THE WORLD. DURING THE FAMINE, SHE TOLD US TO OPEN OUR GATES AND ASK NEIGHBORING COMMUNITIES FOR HELP. PEOPLE NEARLY DIED BECAUSE WE REFUSED TO.
SHE WAS *RIGHT* TO REJECT KYOSHI ISLAND'S ISOLATIONISM. I DIDN'T UNDERSTAND IT THEN, BUT I DO NOW.
THE AVATAR *COULD* HAVE HIDDEN HIMSELF AWAY. HE COULD HAVE REFUSED TO INVOLVE HIMSELF IN THE WORLD'S PROBLEMS, BUT HE DIDN'T. HE WENT BACK OUT THERE TO *HELP* PEOPLE.
IT *IS* HIS JOB TO HELP PEOPLE.
IT SHOULD BE *OUR* JOB AS WELL.

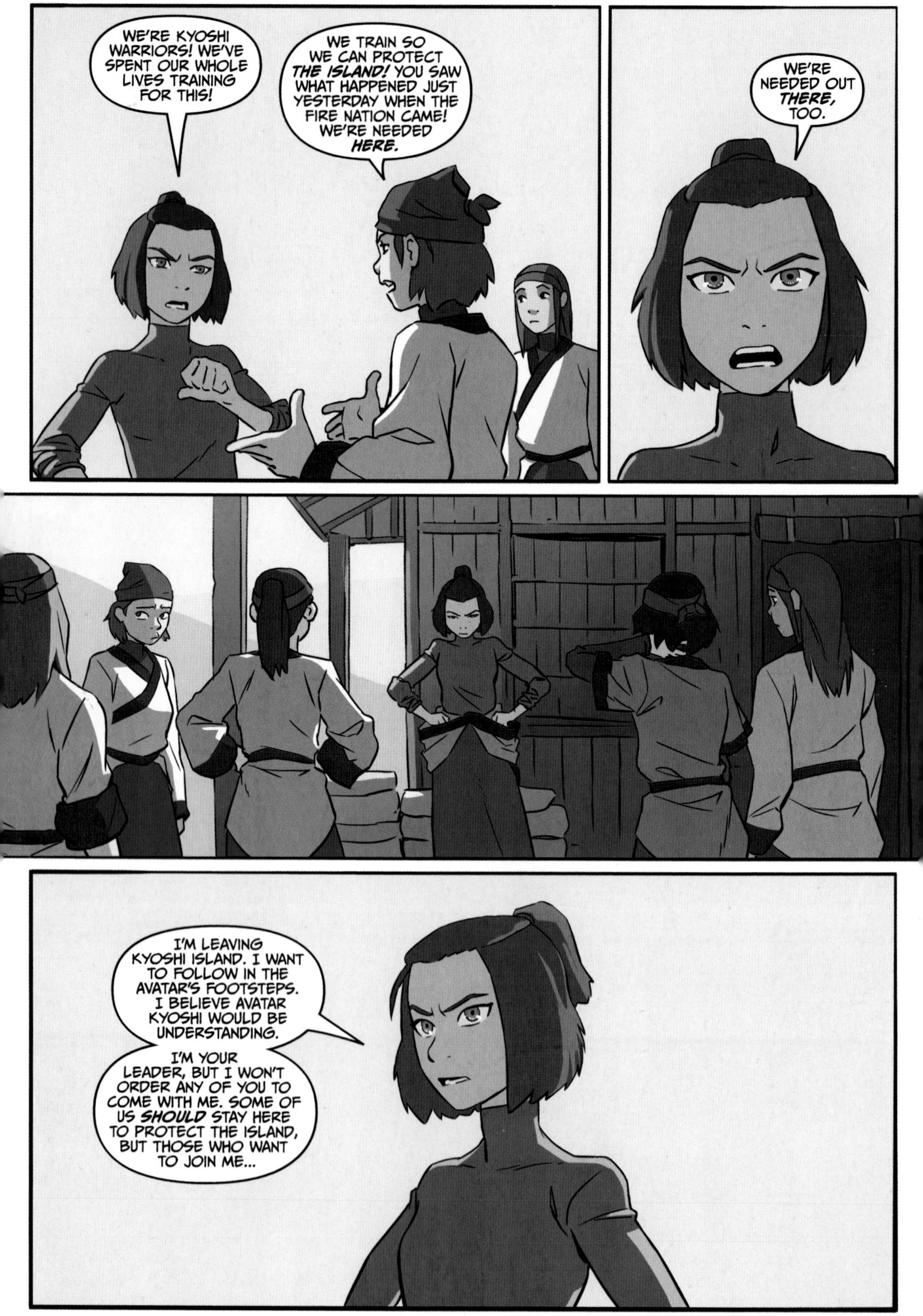
WE'RE KYOSHI WARRIORS! WE'VE SPENT OUR WHOLE LIVES TRAINING FOR THIS!
WE TRAIN SO WE CAN PROTECT *THE ISLAND!* YOU SAW WHAT HAPPENED JUST YESTERDAY WHEN THE FIRE NATION CAME! WE'RE NEEDED *HERE.*
WE'RE NEEDED OUT *THERE,* TOO.
I'M LEAVING KYOSHI ISLAND. I WANT TO FOLLOW IN THE AVATAR'S FOOTSTEPS. I BELIEVE AVATAR KYOSHI WOULD BE UNDERSTANDING.
I'M YOUR LEADER, BUT I WON'T ORDER ANY OF YOU TO COME WITH ME. SOME OF US *SHOULD* STAY HERE TO PROTECT THE ISLAND, BUT THOSE WHO WANT TO JOIN ME...

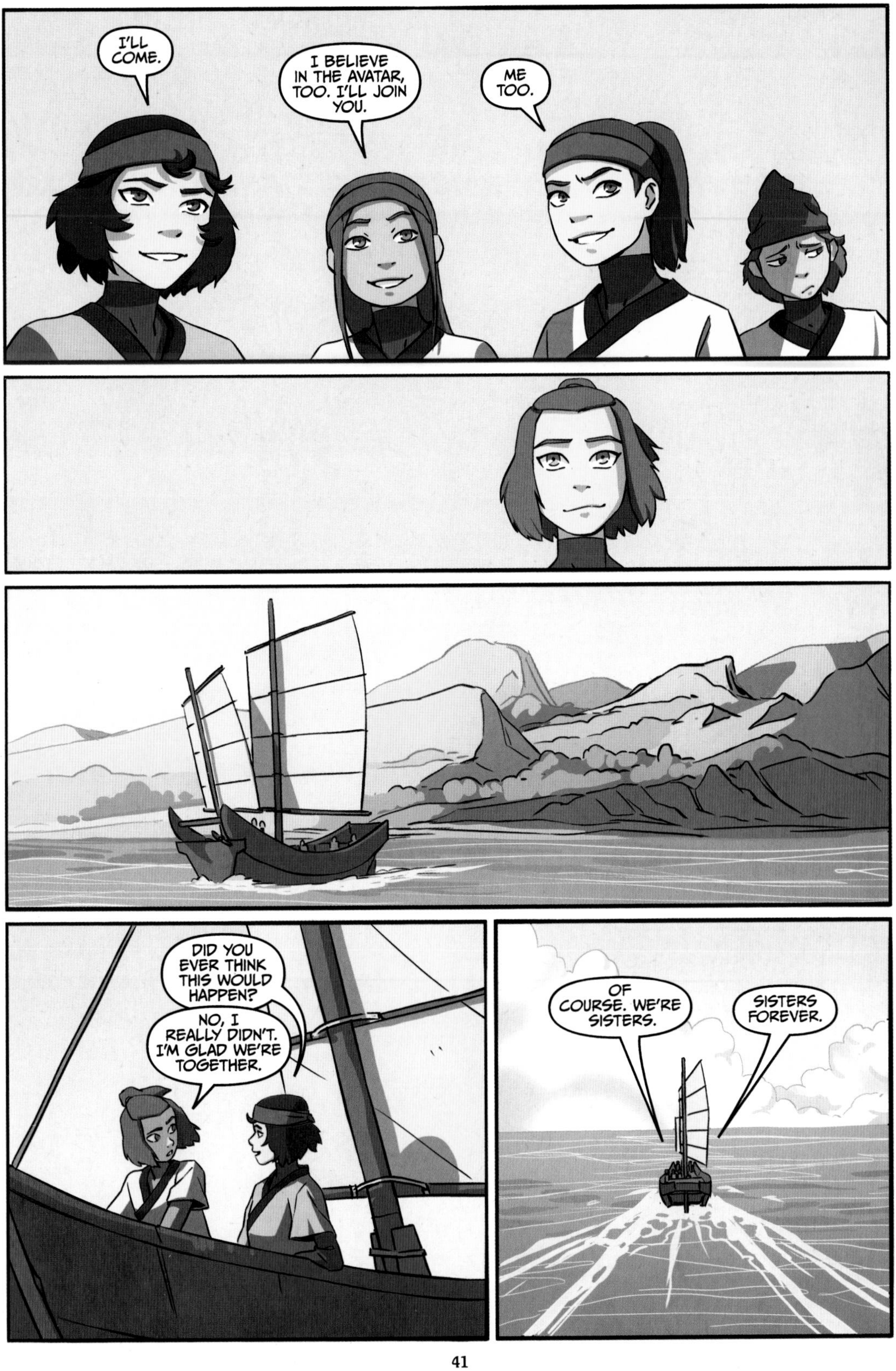
I'LL COME.
I BELIEVE IN THE AVATAR, TOO. I'LL JOIN YOU.
ME TOO.
DID YOU EVER THINK THIS WOULD HAPPEN?
NO, I REALLY DIDN'T. I'M GLAD WE'RE TOGETHER.
OF COURSE. WE'RE SISTERS.
SISTERS FOREVER.

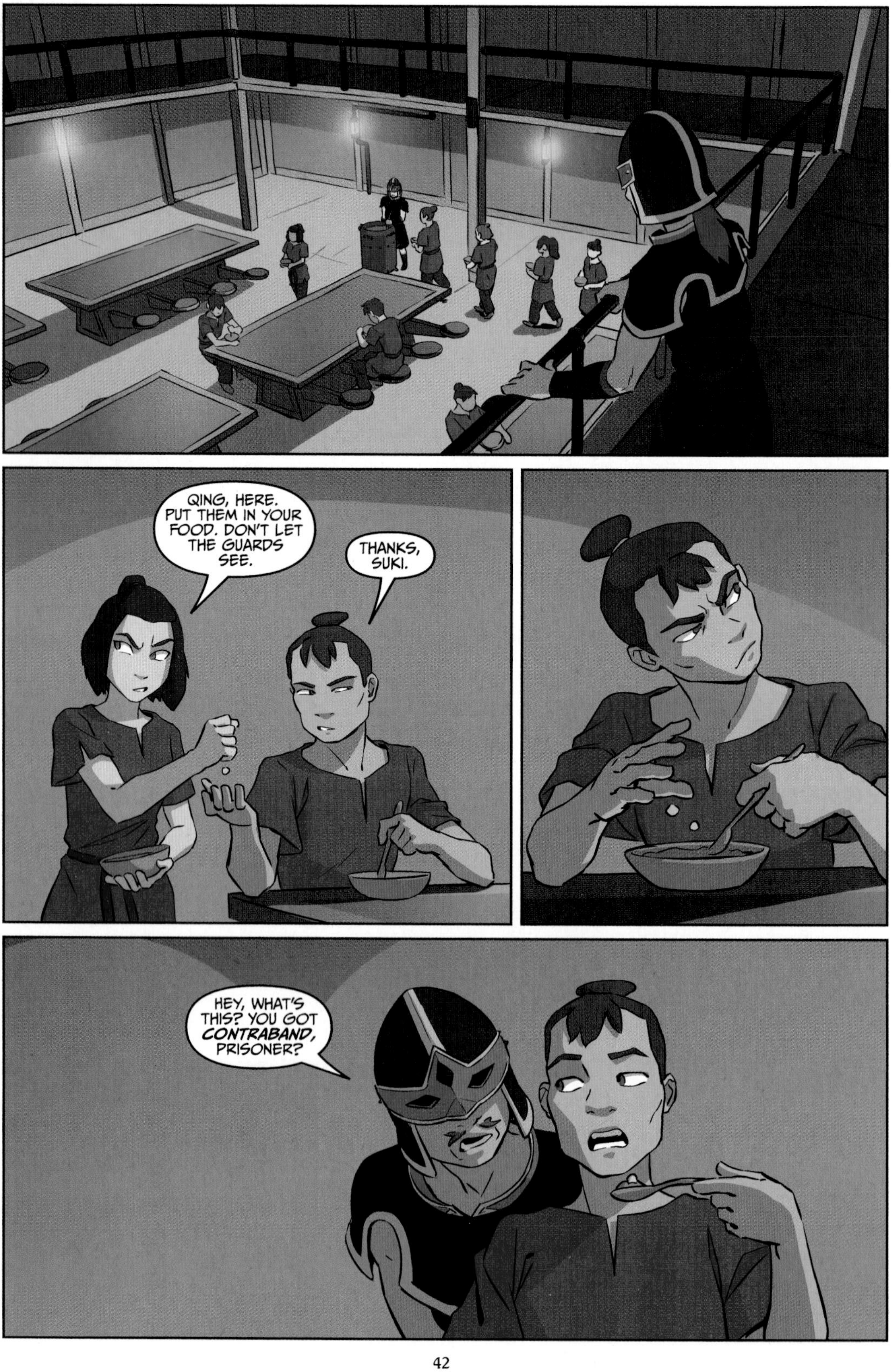
QING, HERE. PUT THEM IN YOUR FOOD. DON'T LET THE GUARDS SEE.
THANKS, SUKI.
HEY, WHAT'S THIS? YOU GOT ***CONTRABAND***, PRISONER?

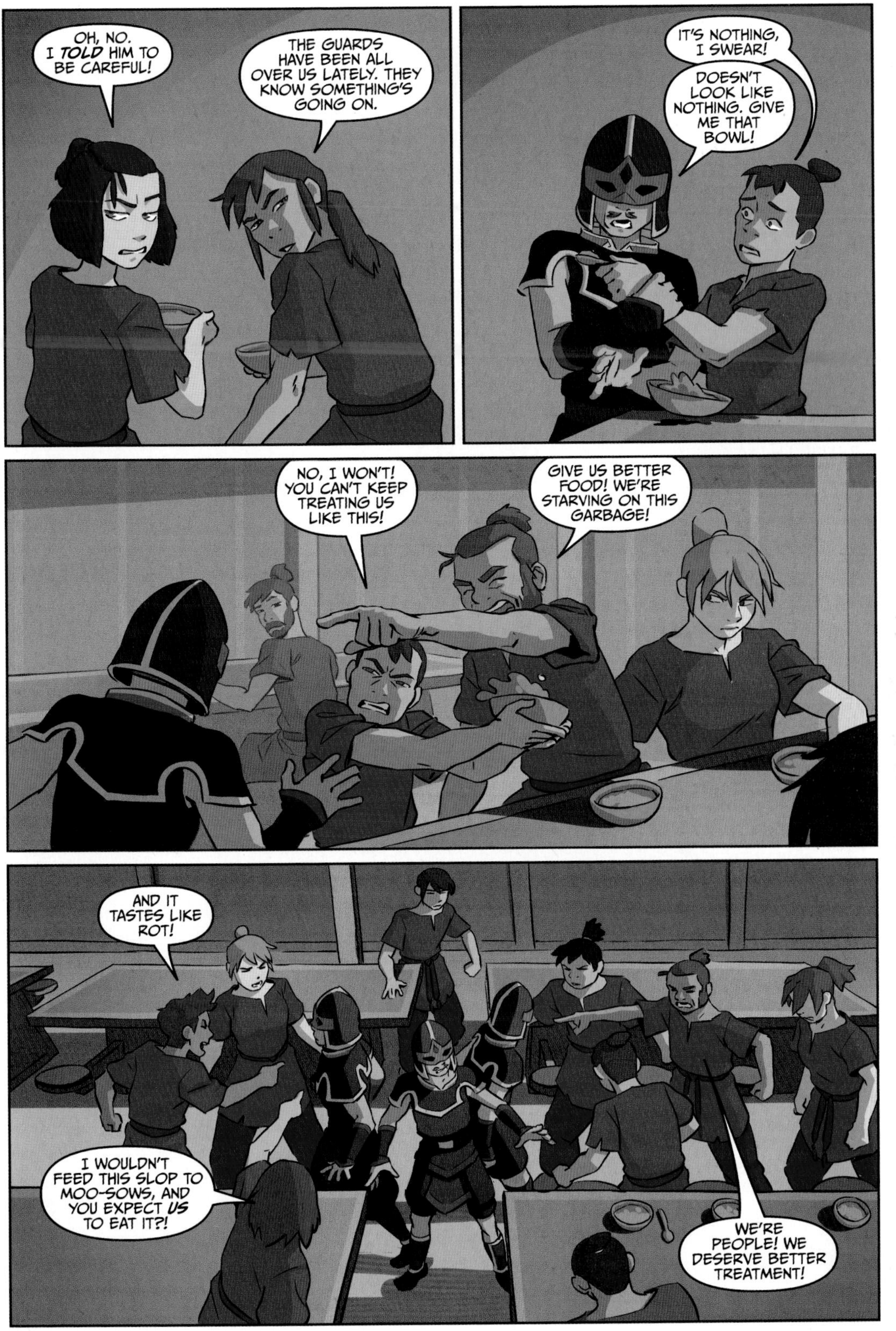
OH, NO. I TOLD HIM TO BE CAREFUL!
THE GUARDS HAVE BEEN ALL OVER US LATELY. THEY KNOW SOMETHING'S GOING ON.
IT'S NOTHING, I SWEAR!
DOESN'T LOOK LIKE NOTHING. GIVE ME THAT BOWL!
NO, I WON'T! YOU CAN'T KEEP TREATING US LIKE THIS!
GIVE US BETTER FOOD! WE'RE STARVING ON THIS GARBAGE!
AND IT TASTES LIKE ROT!
I WOULDN'T FEED THIS SLOP TO MOO-SOWS, AND YOU EXPECT US TO EAT IT?!
WE'RE PEOPLE! WE DESERVE BETTER TREATMENT!

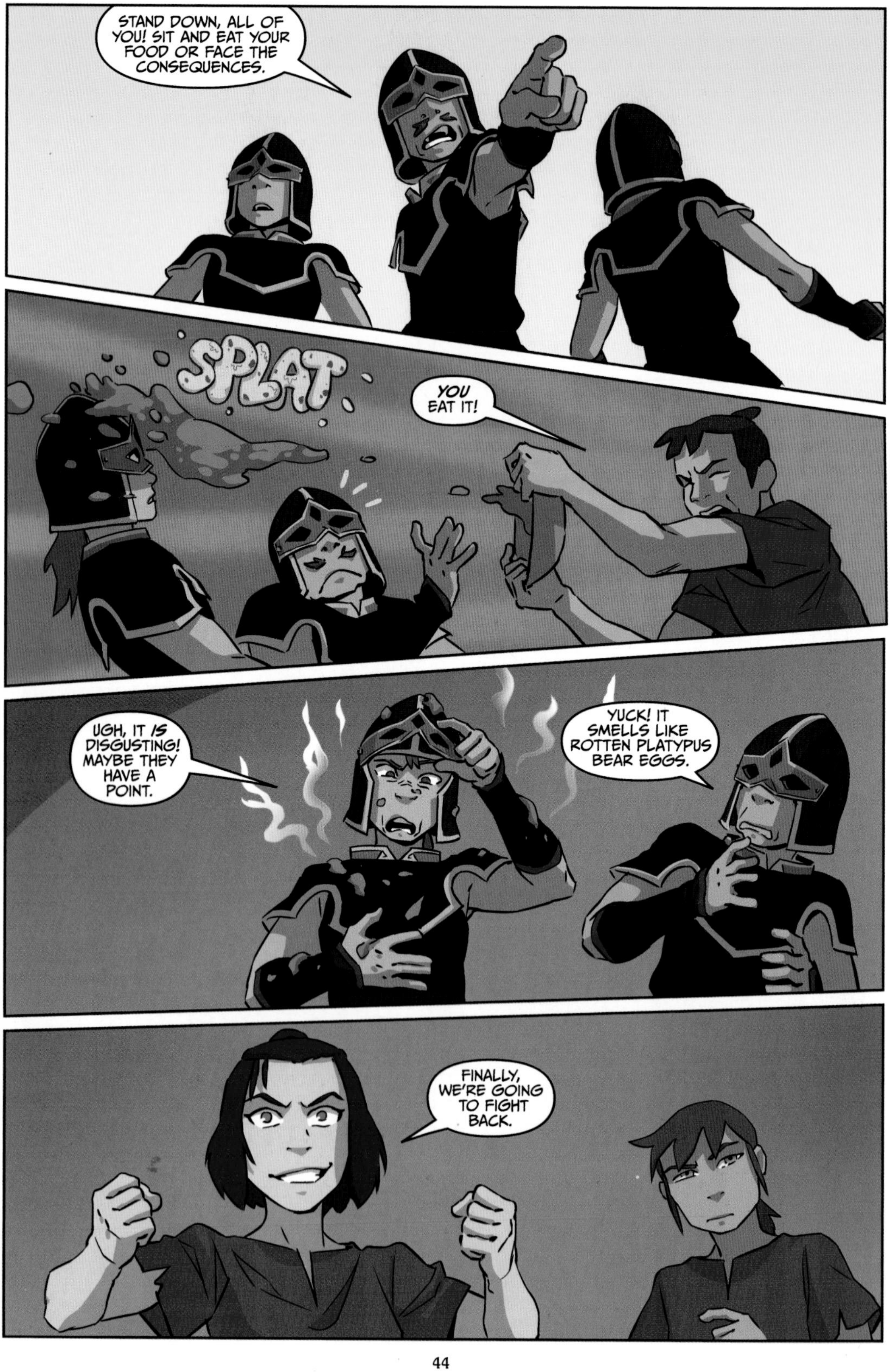

STAND DOWN, ALL OF YOU! SIT AND EAT YOUR FOOD OR FACE THE CONSEQUENCES.
SPLAT
YOU EAT IT!
UGH, IT IS DISGUSTING! MAYBE THEY HAVE A POINT.
YUCK! IT SMELLS LIKE ROTTEN PLATYPUS BEAR EGGS.
FINALLY, WE'RE GOING TO FIGHT BACK.

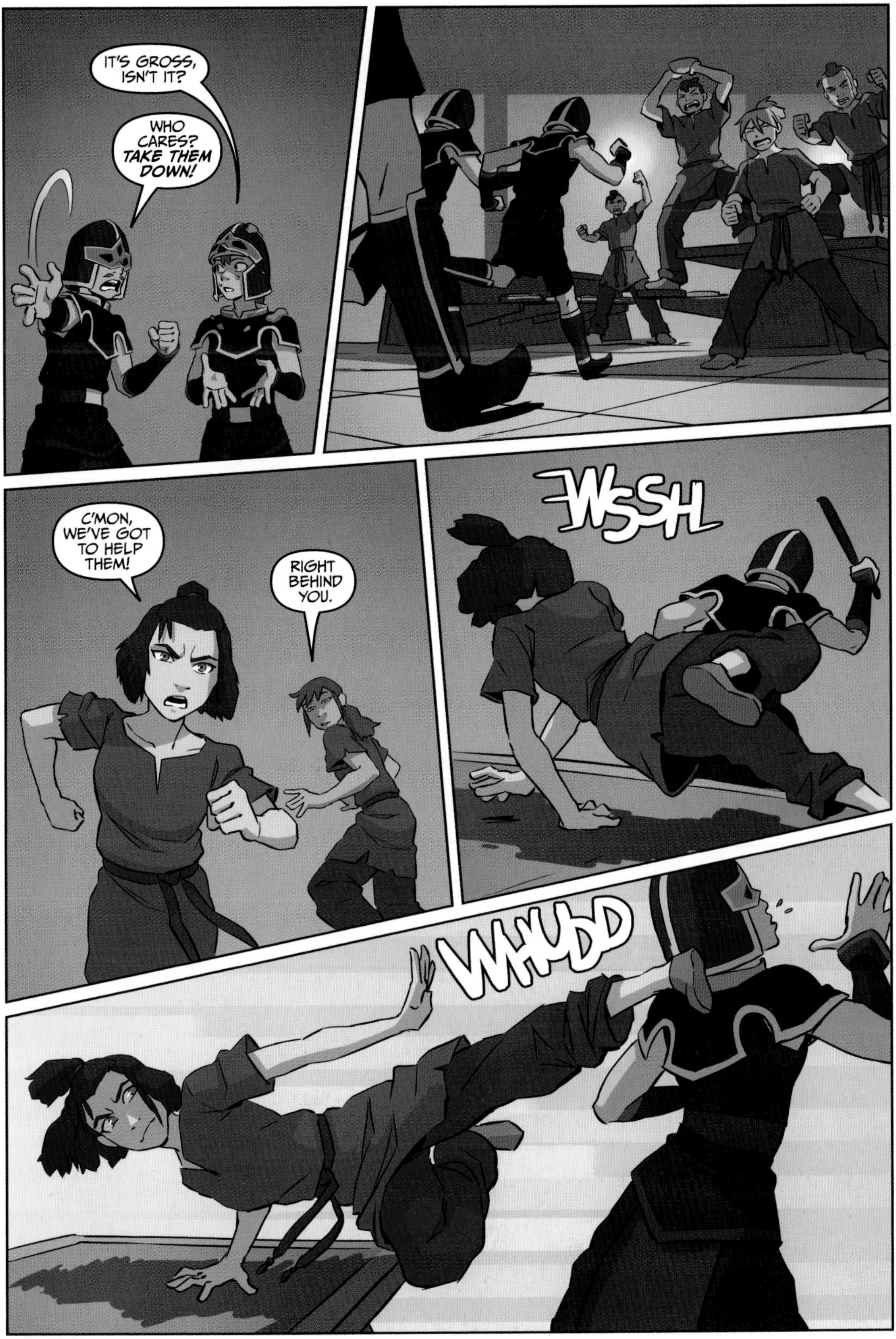
IT'S GROSS, ISN'T IT?
WHO CARES? TAKE THEM DOWN!
C'MON, WE'VE GOT TO HELP THEM!
RIGHT BEHIND YOU.
FWSSH
WHUDD

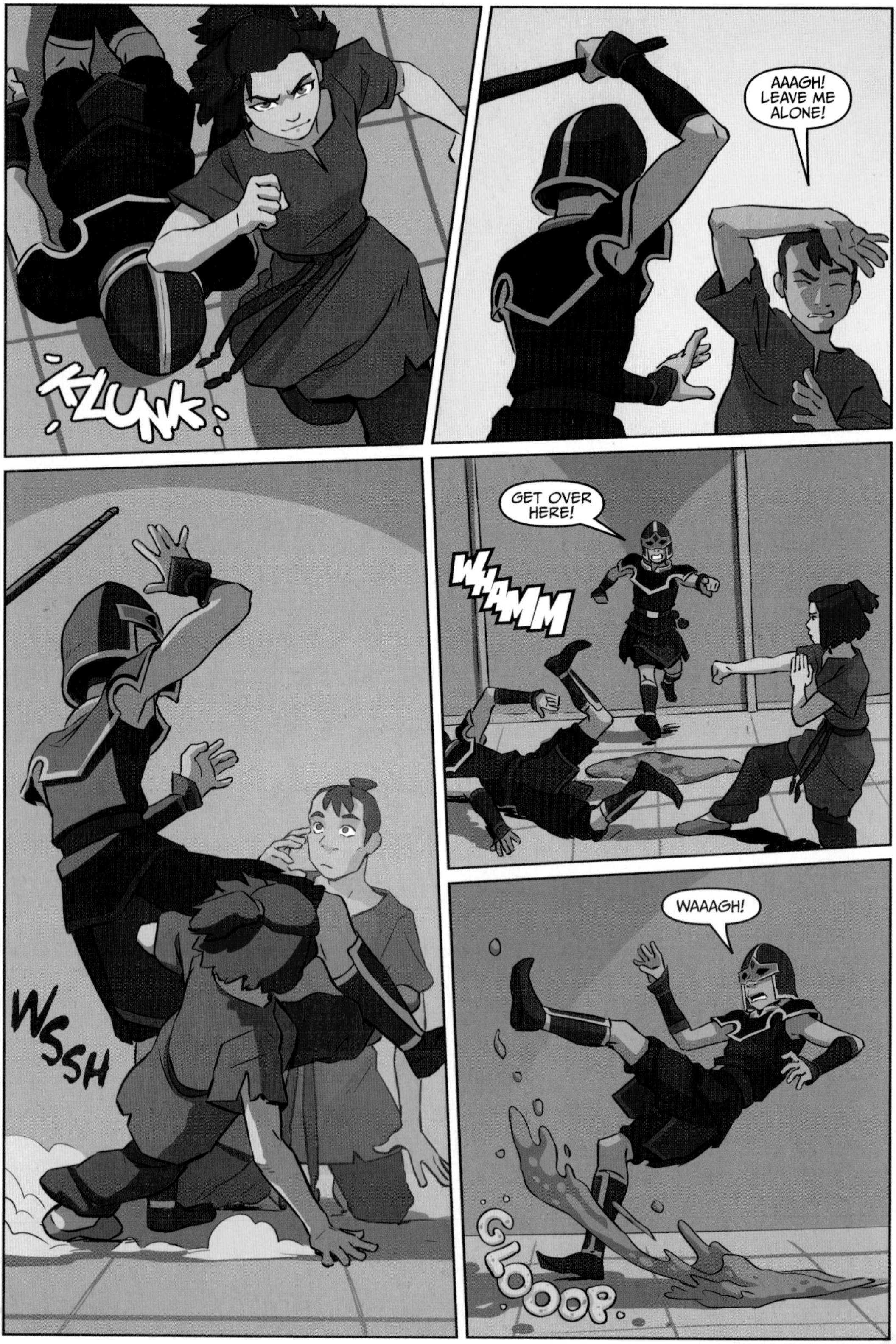
KLUNK
AAAGH! LEAVE ME ALONE!
WSSH
GET OVER HERE!
WHAMM
WAAAGH!
GLOOOP

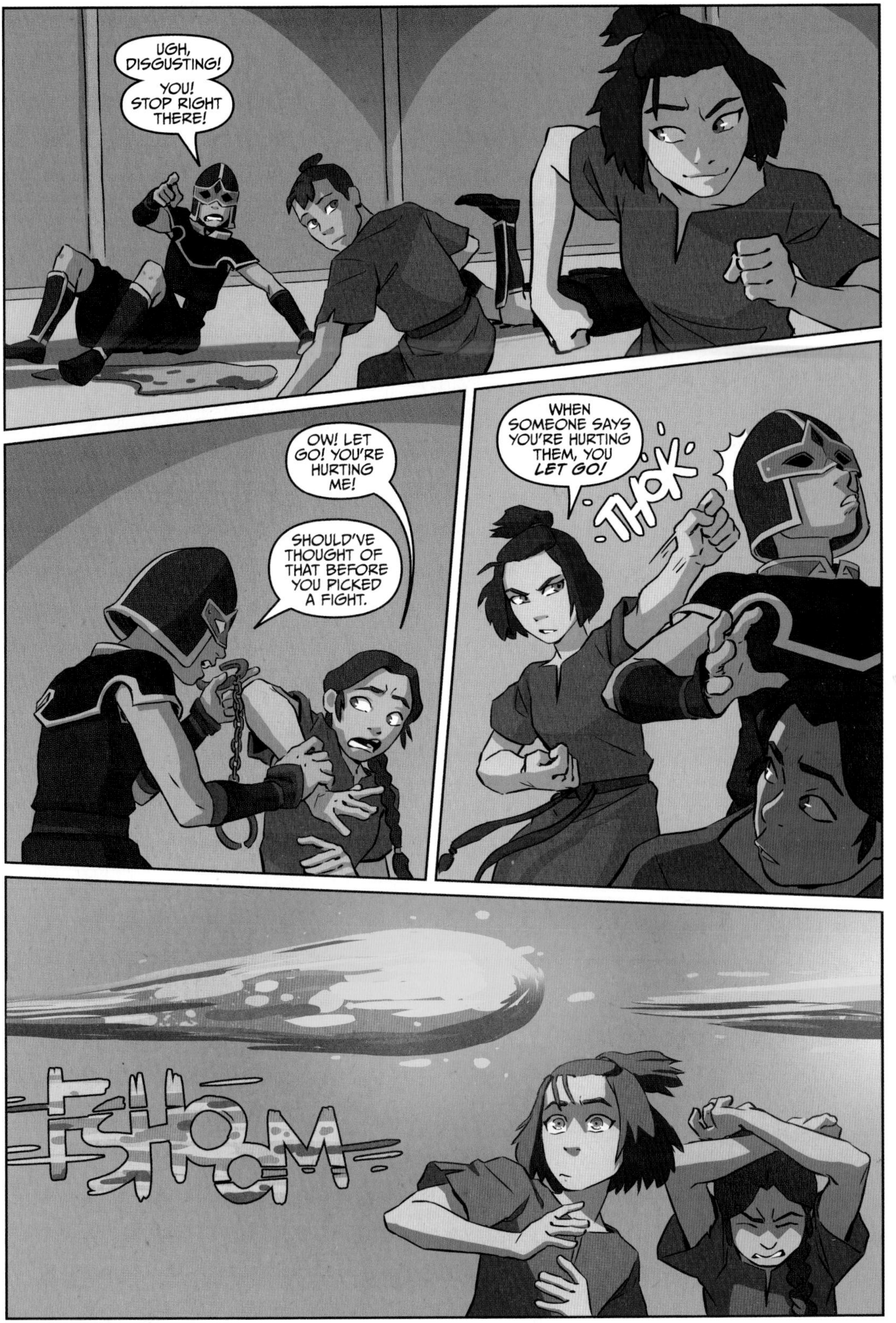
UGH, DISGUSTING!
YOU! STOP RIGHT THERE!
OW! LET GO! YOU'RE HURTING ME!
SHOULD'VE THOUGHT OF THAT BEFORE YOU PICKED A FIGHT.
WHEN SOMEONE SAYS YOU'RE HURTING THEM, YOU LET GO!
THOK
FSHOOM

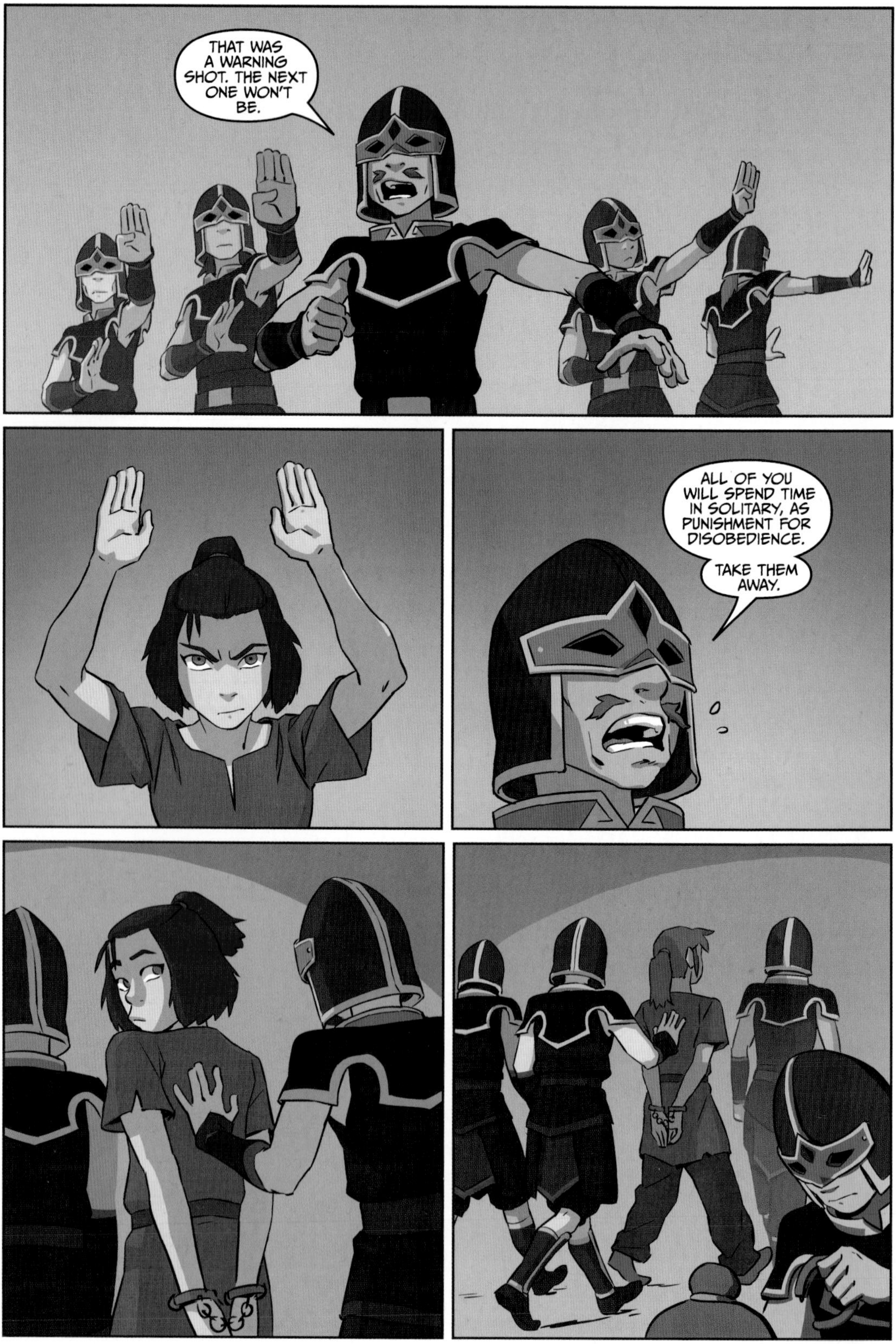
THAT WAS A WARNING SHOT. THE NEXT ONE WON'T BE.
ALL OF YOU WILL SPEND TIME IN SOLITARY, AS PUNISHMENT FOR DISOBEDIENCE.
TAKE THEM AWAY.

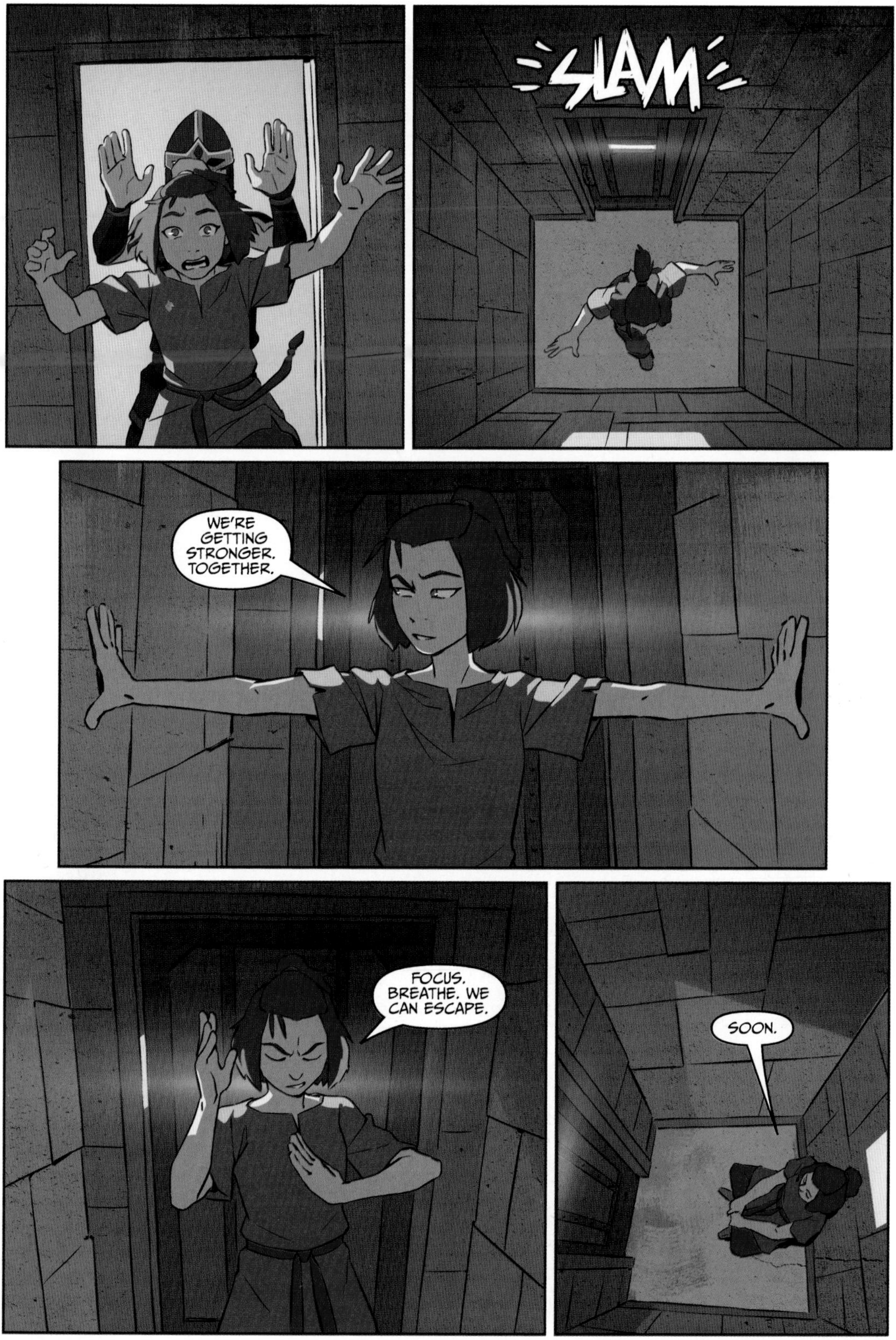
SLAM
WE'RE GETTING STRONGER. TOGETHER.
FOCUS. BREATHE. WE CAN ESCAPE.
SOON.

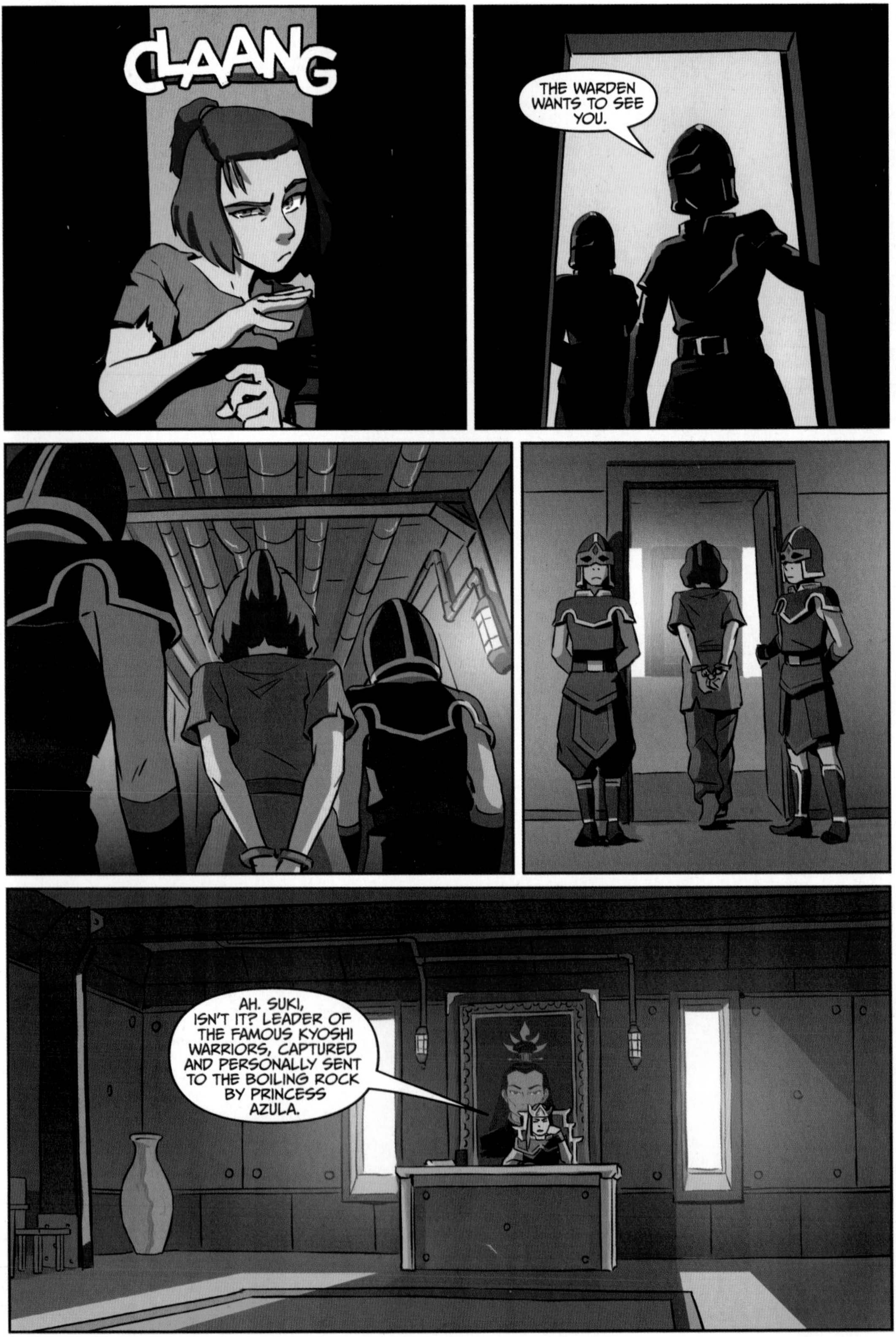
CLAANG
THE WARDEN WANTS TO SEE YOU.
AH. SUKI, ISN'T IT? LEADER OF THE FAMOUS KYOSHI WARRIORS, CAPTURED AND PERSONALLY SENT TO THE BOILING ROCK BY PRINCESS AZULA.

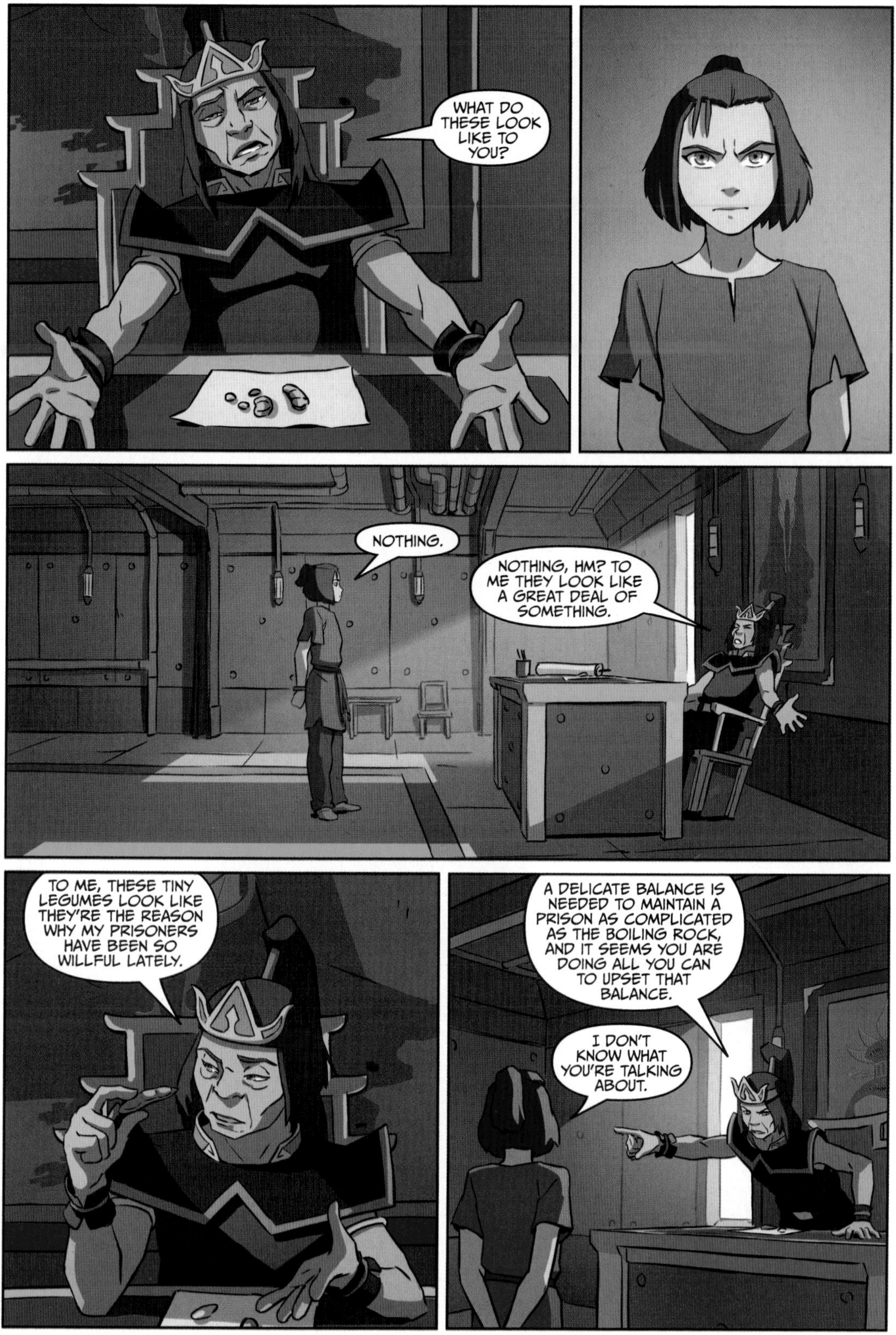
WHAT DO THESE LOOK LIKE TO YOU?
NOTHING.
NOTHING, HM? TO ME THEY LOOK LIKE A GREAT DEAL OF SOMETHING.
TO ME, THESE TINY LEGUMES LOOK LIKE THEY'RE THE REASON WHY MY PRISONERS HAVE BEEN SO WILLFUL LATELY.
A DELICATE BALANCE IS NEEDED TO MAINTAIN A PRISON AS COMPLICATED AS THE BOILING ROCK, AND IT SEEMS YOU ARE DOING ALL YOU CAN TO UPSET THAT BALANCE.
I DON'T KNOW WHAT YOU'RE TALKING ABOUT.

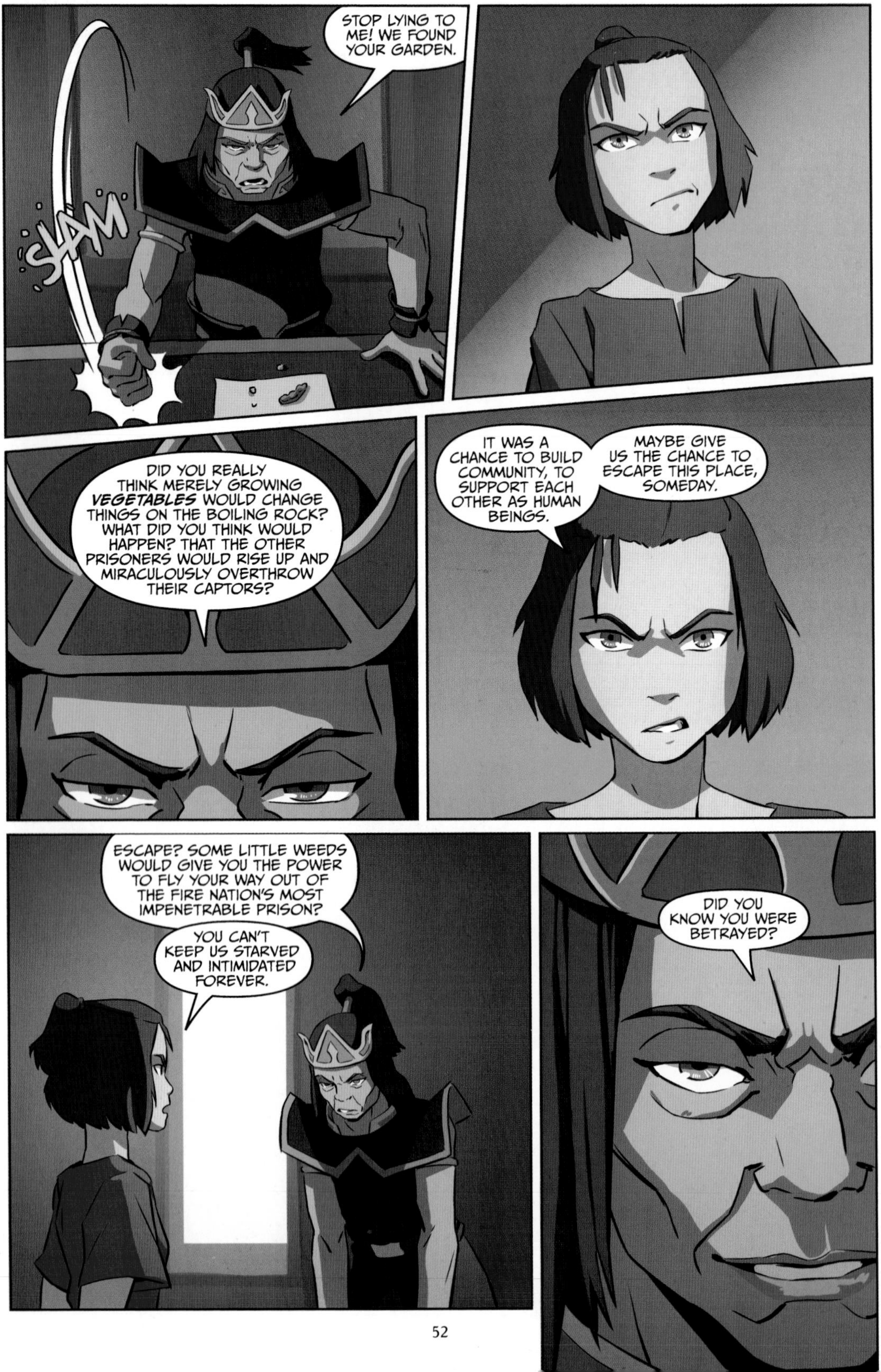
STOP LYING TO ME! WE FOUND YOUR GARDEN.
SLAM
DID YOU REALLY THINK MERELY GROWING *VEGETABLES* WOULD CHANGE THINGS ON THE BOILING ROCK? WHAT DID YOU THINK WOULD HAPPEN? THAT THE OTHER PRISONERS WOULD RISE UP AND MIRACULOUSLY OVERTHROW THEIR CAPTORS?
IT WAS A CHANCE TO BUILD COMMUNITY, TO SUPPORT EACH OTHER AS HUMAN BEINGS.
MAYBE GIVE US THE CHANCE TO ESCAPE THIS PLACE, SOMEDAY.
ESCAPE? SOME LITTLE WEEDS WOULD GIVE YOU THE POWER TO FLY YOUR WAY OUT OF THE FIRE NATION'S MOST IMPENETRABLE PRISON?
YOU CAN'T KEEP US STARVED AND INTIMIDATED FOREVER.
DID YOU KNOW YOU WERE BETRAYED?

YOU'RE *LYING.*

ONE OF YOUR OWN, ONE OF THOSE FELLOW HUMAN BEINGS YOU'VE BEEN RISKING YOUR NECK TO FEED, CAME TO ME AND GAVE YOU UP. YOUR GARDEN, YOUR SECRET PASSAGE THROUGH THE LAUNDRY ROOM, ALL YOUR TOOLS. ALL GONE NOW.

IT'S A COMMON MISTAKE, COMING TO BOILING ROCK PRISON AND THINKING YOU'VE MADE FRIENDS HERE. FRIENDS *WOULD* MAKE SURVIVING A LOT EASIER.

BUT YOU HAVE NO FRIENDS HERE. YOU'RE COMPLETELY ALONE.

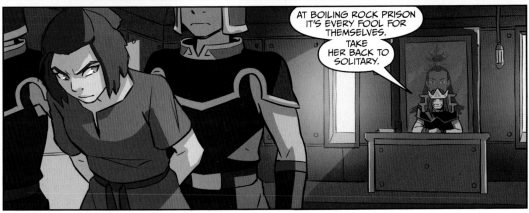

AT BOILING ROCK PRISON IT'S EVERY FOOL FOR THEMSELVES.

TAKE HER BACK TO SOLITARY.

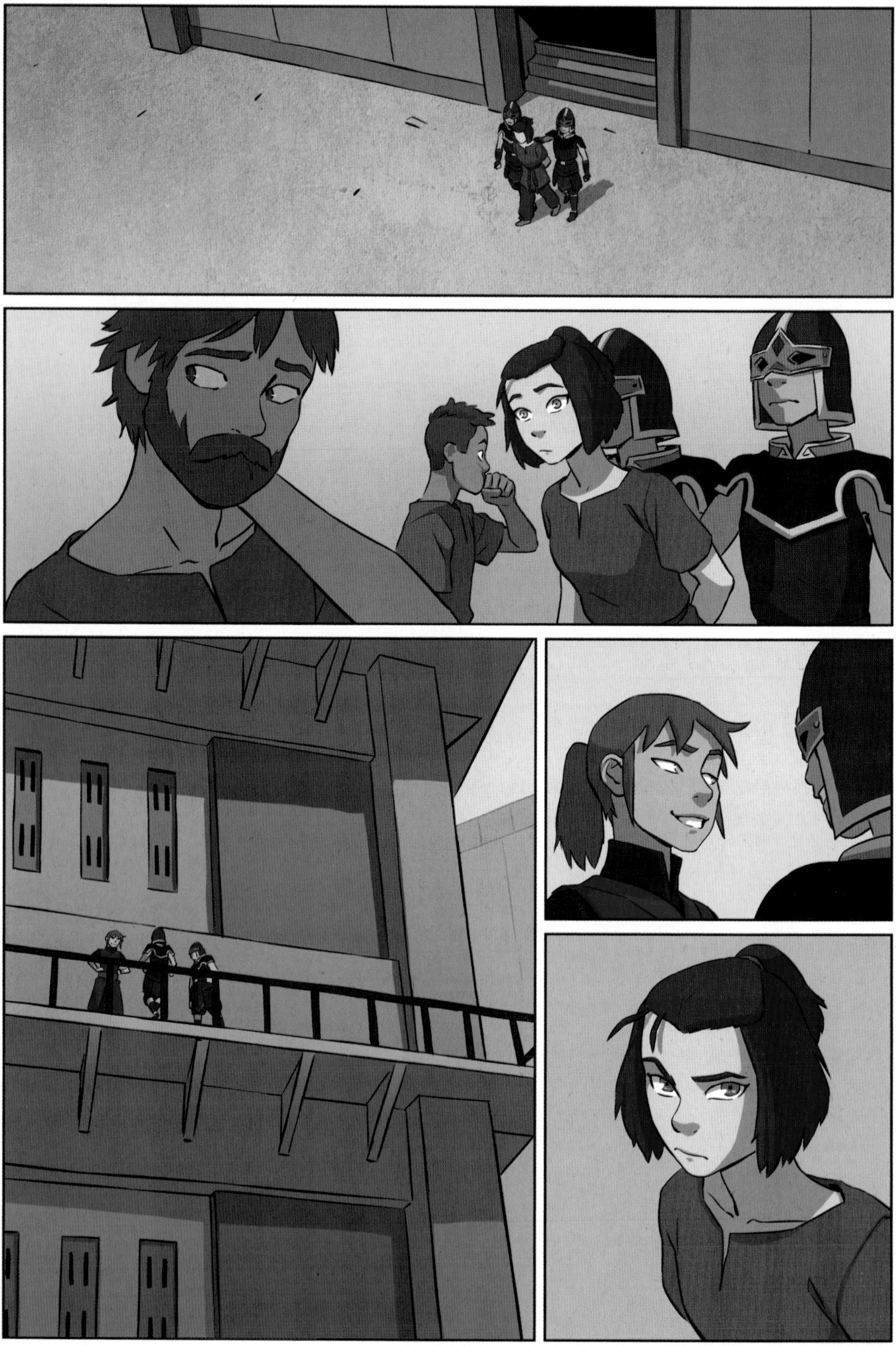

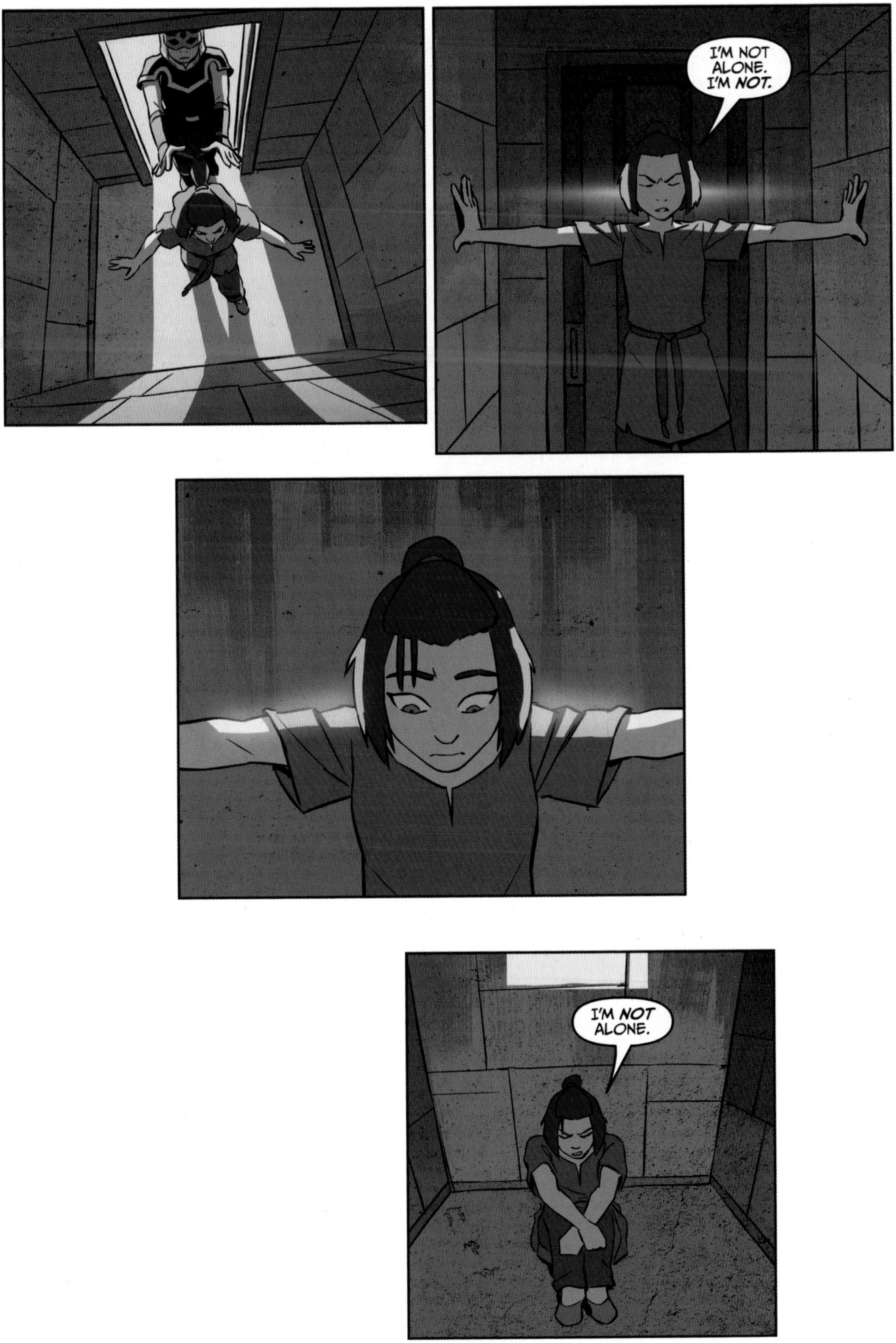
I'M NOT ALONE. I'M NOT.
I'M NOT ALONE.

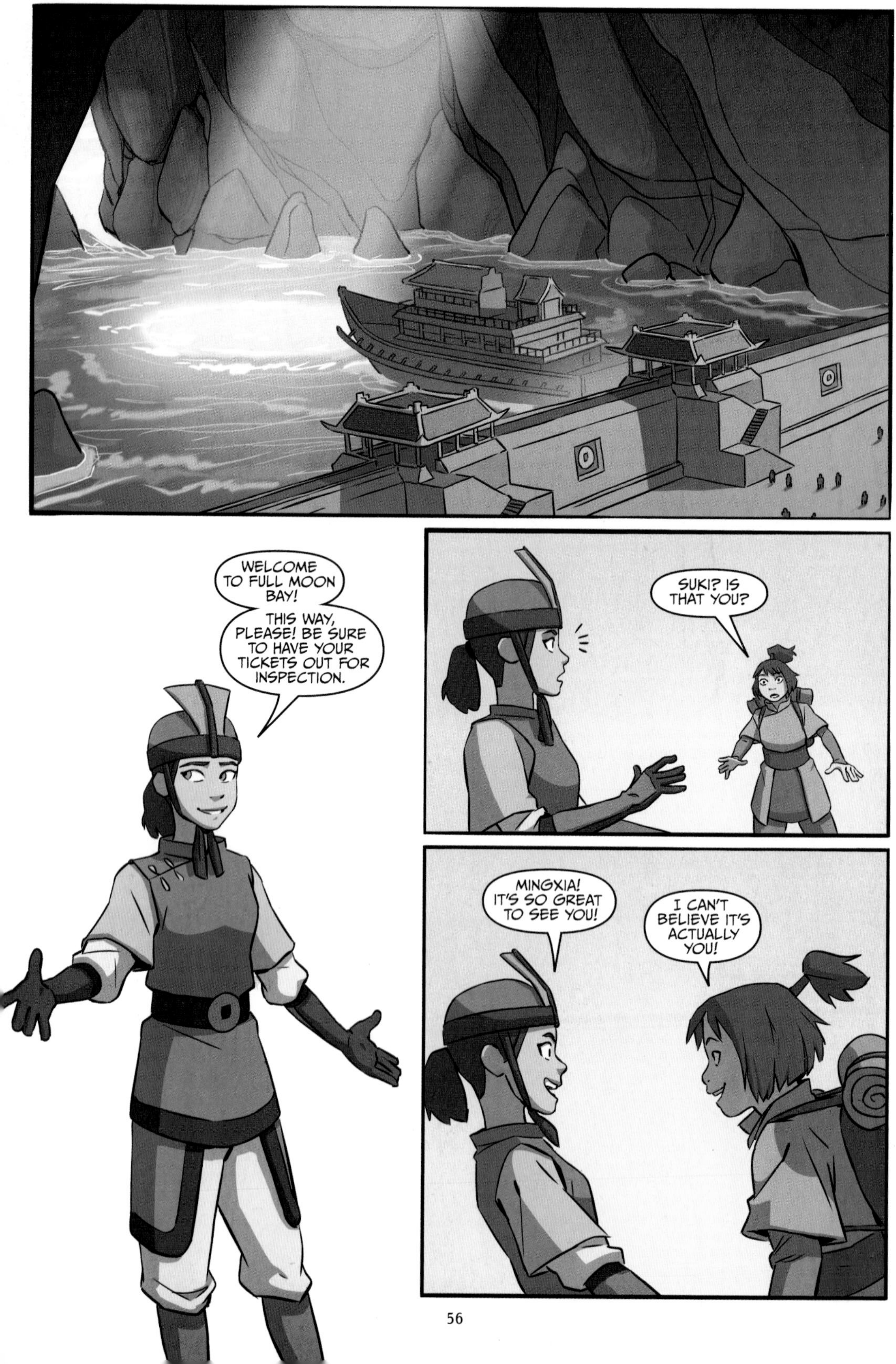
WELCOME TO FULL MOON BAY!
THIS WAY, PLEASE! BE SURE TO HAVE YOUR TICKETS OUT FOR INSPECTION.
SUKI? IS THAT YOU?
MINGXIA! IT'S SO GREAT TO SEE YOU!
I CAN'T BELIEVE IT'S ACTUALLY YOU!

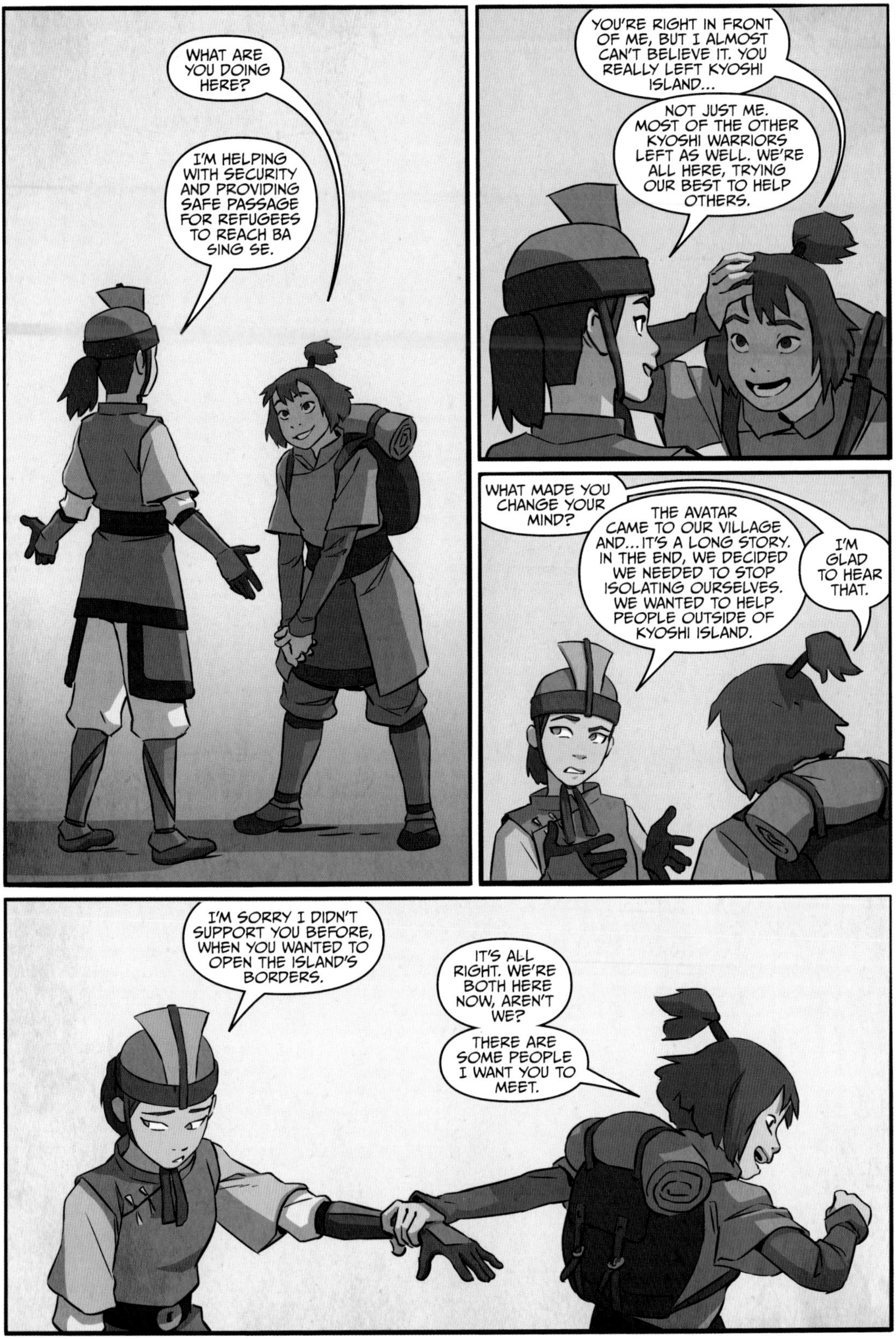
WHAT ARE YOU DOING HERE?
I'M HELPING WITH SECURITY AND PROVIDING SAFE PASSAGE FOR REFUGEES TO REACH BA SING SE.
YOU'RE RIGHT IN FRONT OF ME, BUT I ALMOST CAN'T BELIEVE IT. YOU REALLY LEFT KYOSHI ISLAND...
NOT JUST ME. MOST OF THE OTHER KYOSHI WARRIORS LEFT AS WELL. WE'RE ALL HERE, TRYING OUR BEST TO HELP OTHERS.
WHAT MADE YOU CHANGE YOUR MIND?
THE AVATAR CAME TO OUR VILLAGE AND... IT'S A LONG STORY. IN THE END, WE DECIDED WE NEEDED TO STOP ISOLATING OURSELVES. WE WANTED TO HELP PEOPLE OUTSIDE OF KYOSHI ISLAND.
I'M GLAD TO HEAR THAT.
I'M SORRY I DIDN'T SUPPORT YOU BEFORE, WHEN YOU WANTED TO OPEN THE ISLAND'S BORDERS.
IT'S ALL RIGHT. WE'RE BOTH HERE NOW, AREN'T WE?
THERE ARE SOME PEOPLE I WANT YOU TO MEET.

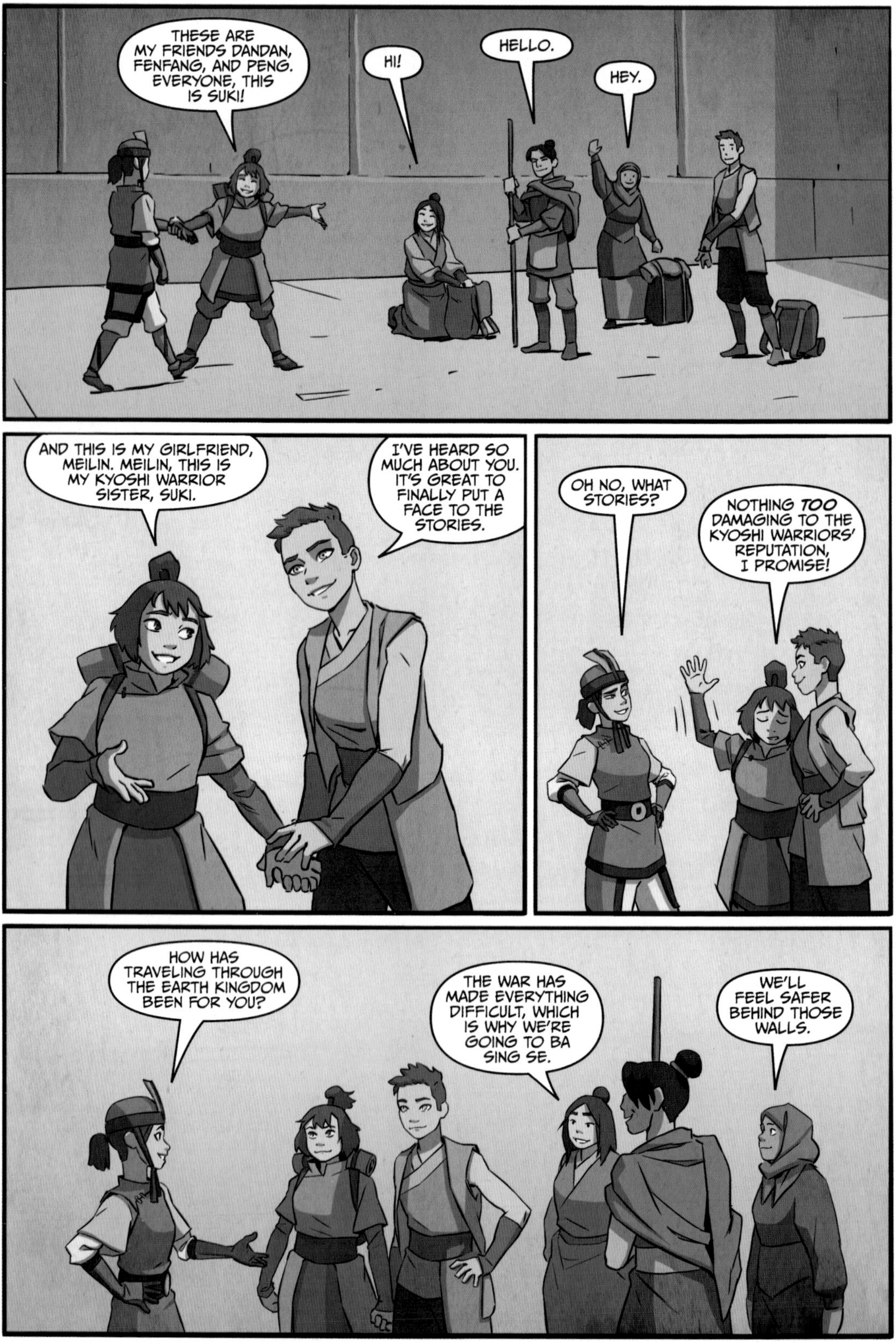
THESE ARE MY FRIENDS DANDAN, FENFANG, AND PENG. EVERYONE, THIS IS SUKI!
HI!
HELLO.
HEY.
AND THIS IS MY GIRLFRIEND, MEILIN. MEILIN, THIS IS MY KYOSHI WARRIOR SISTER, SUKI.
I'VE HEARD SO MUCH ABOUT YOU. IT'S GREAT TO FINALLY PUT A FACE TO THE STORIES.
OH NO, WHAT STORIES?
NOTHING *TOO* DAMAGING TO THE KYOSHI WARRIORS' REPUTATION, I PROMISE!
HOW HAS TRAVELING THROUGH THE EARTH KINGDOM BEEN FOR YOU?
THE WAR HAS MADE EVERYTHING DIFFICULT, WHICH IS WHY WE'RE GOING TO BA SING SE.
WE'LL FEEL SAFER BEHIND THOSE WALLS.

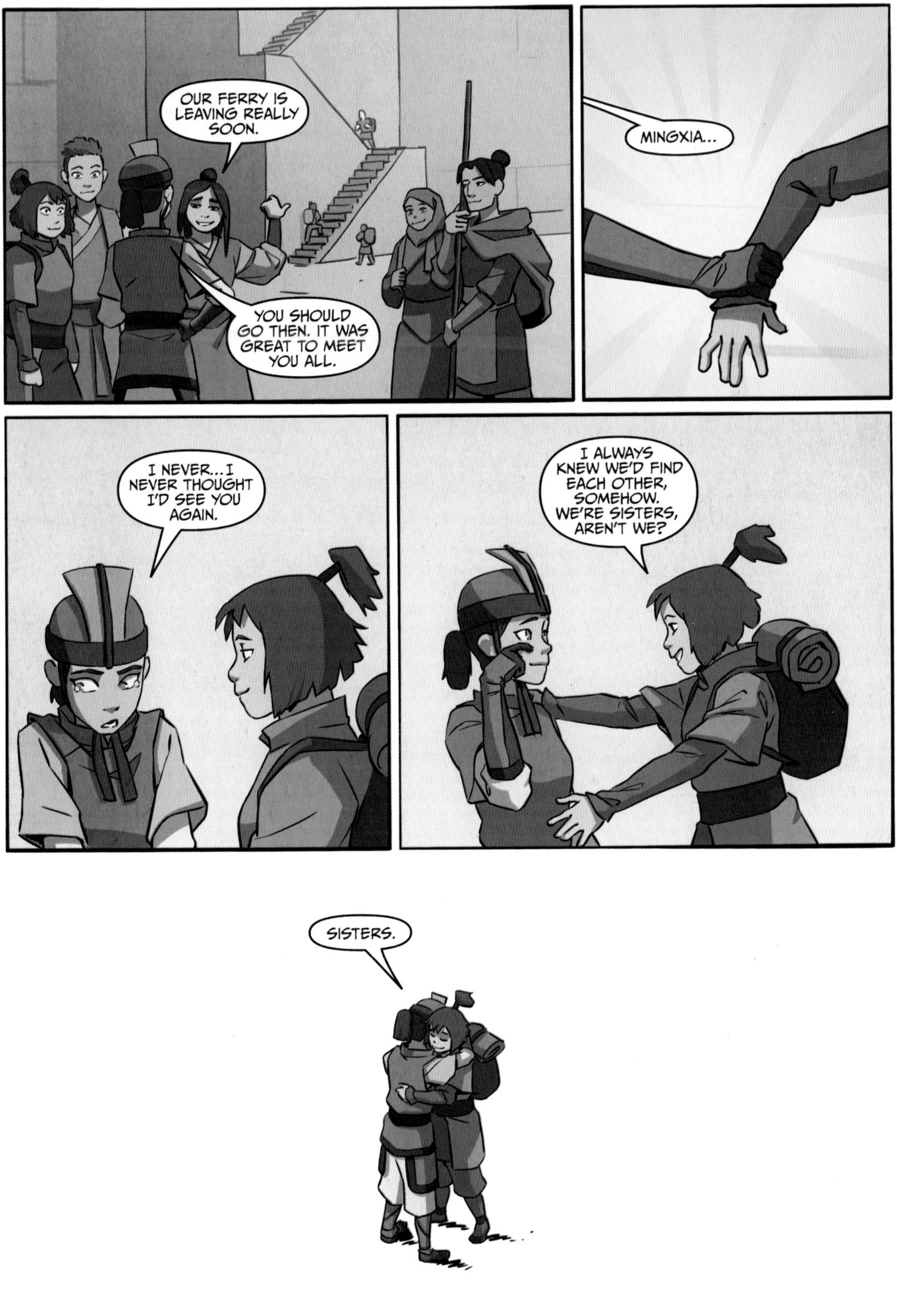
OUR FERRY IS LEAVING REALLY SOON.
YOU SHOULD GO THEN. IT WAS GREAT TO MEET YOU ALL.
MINGXIA...
I NEVER...I NEVER THOUGHT I'D SEE YOU AGAIN.
I ALWAYS KNEW WE'D FIND EACH OTHER, SOMEHOW. WE'RE SISTERS, AREN'T WE?
SISTERS.

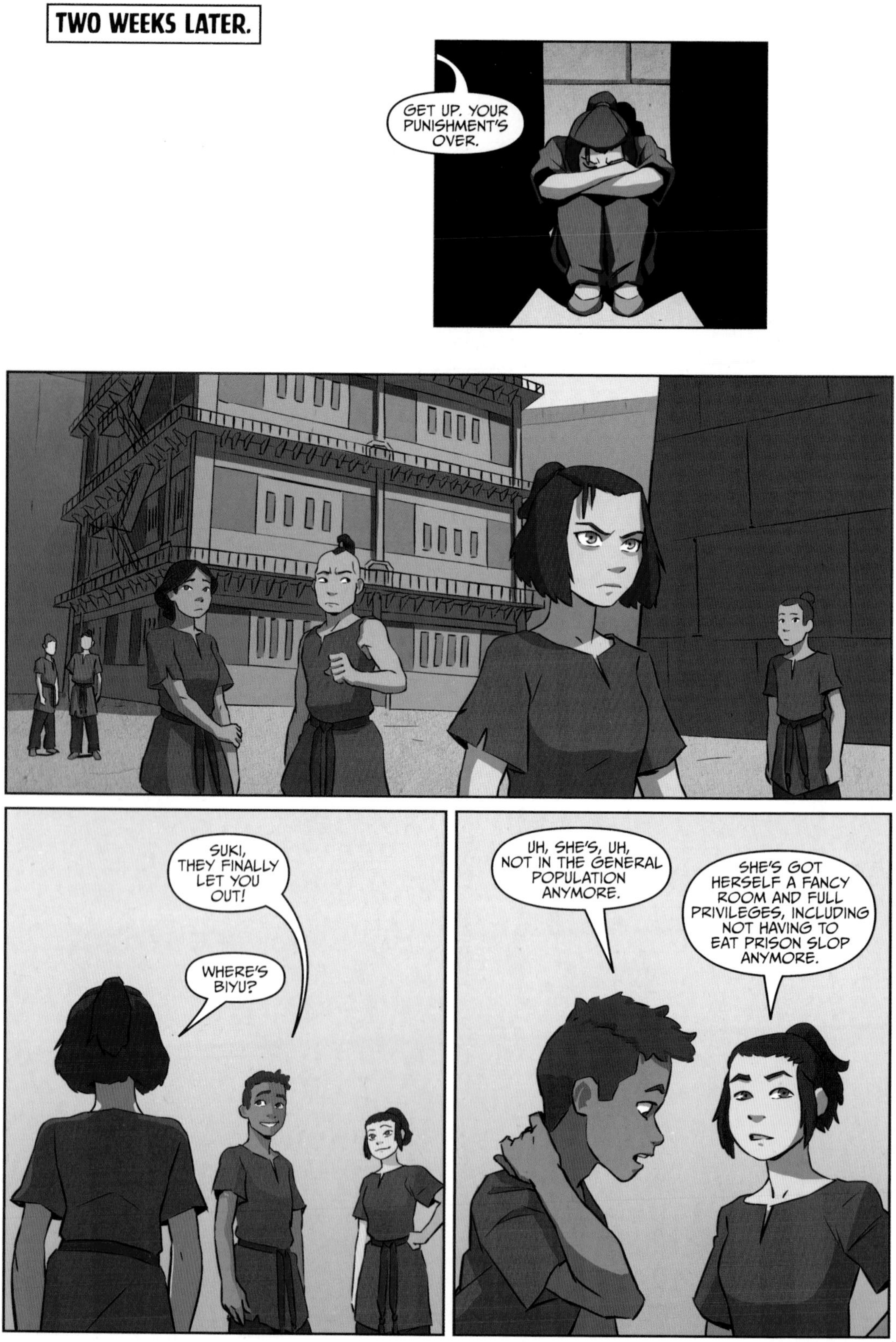
TWO WEEKS LATER.
GET UP. YOUR PUNISHMENT'S OVER.
SUKI, THEY FINALLY LET YOU OUT!
WHERE'S BIYU?
UH, SHE'S, UH, NOT IN THE GENERAL POPULATION ANYMORE.
SHE'S GOT HERSELF A FANCY ROOM AND FULL PRIVILEGES, INCLUDING NOT HAVING TO EAT PRISON SLOP ANYMORE.

AND I WONDER WHAT SHE SAID TO GET THESE PRIVILEGES. ANYONE HAVE A GUESS?

NEVERMIND. WE ALL KNOW.

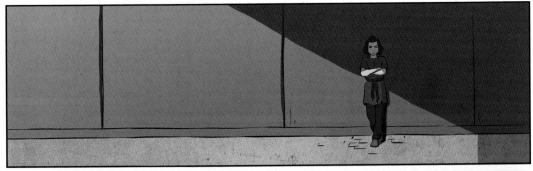

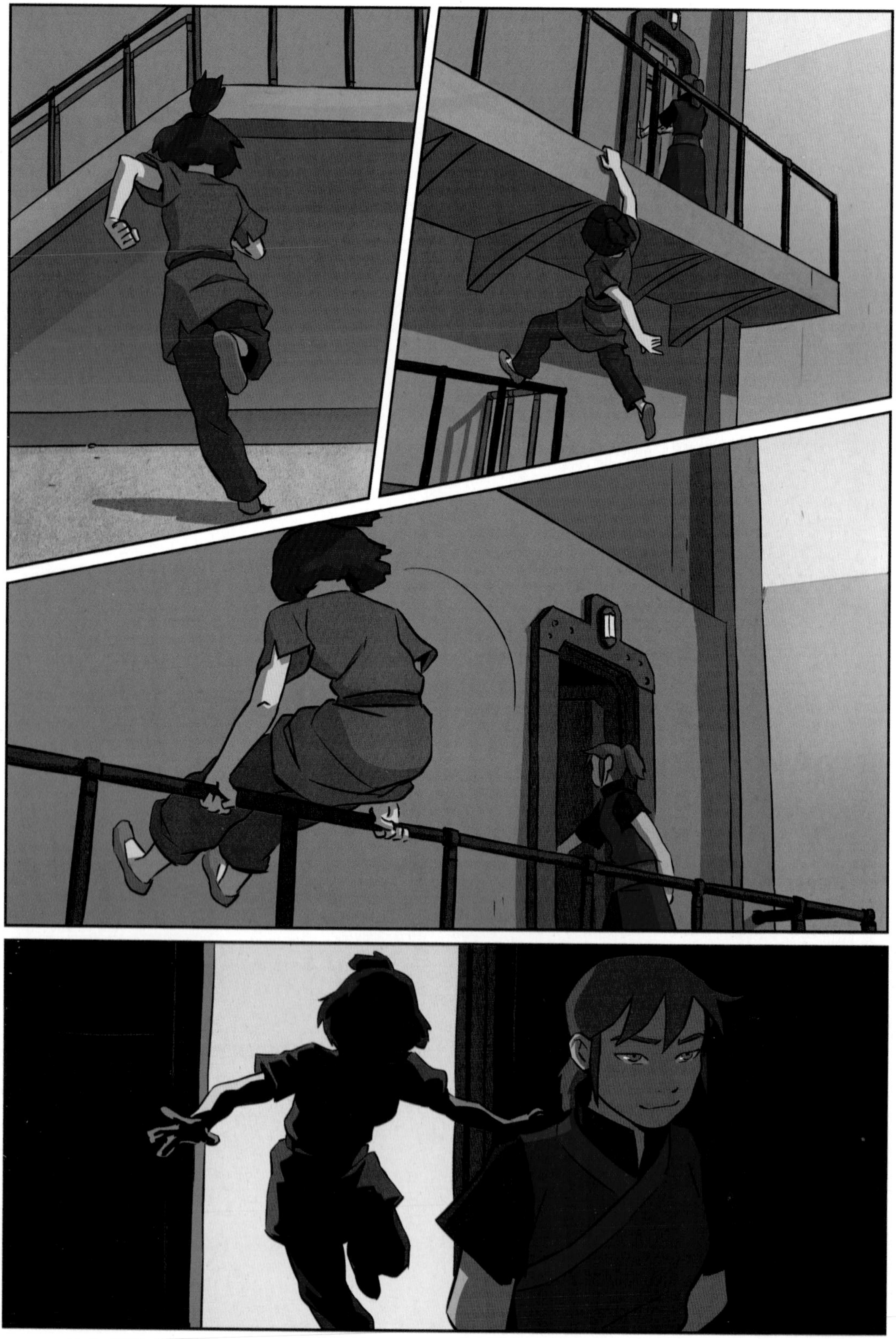

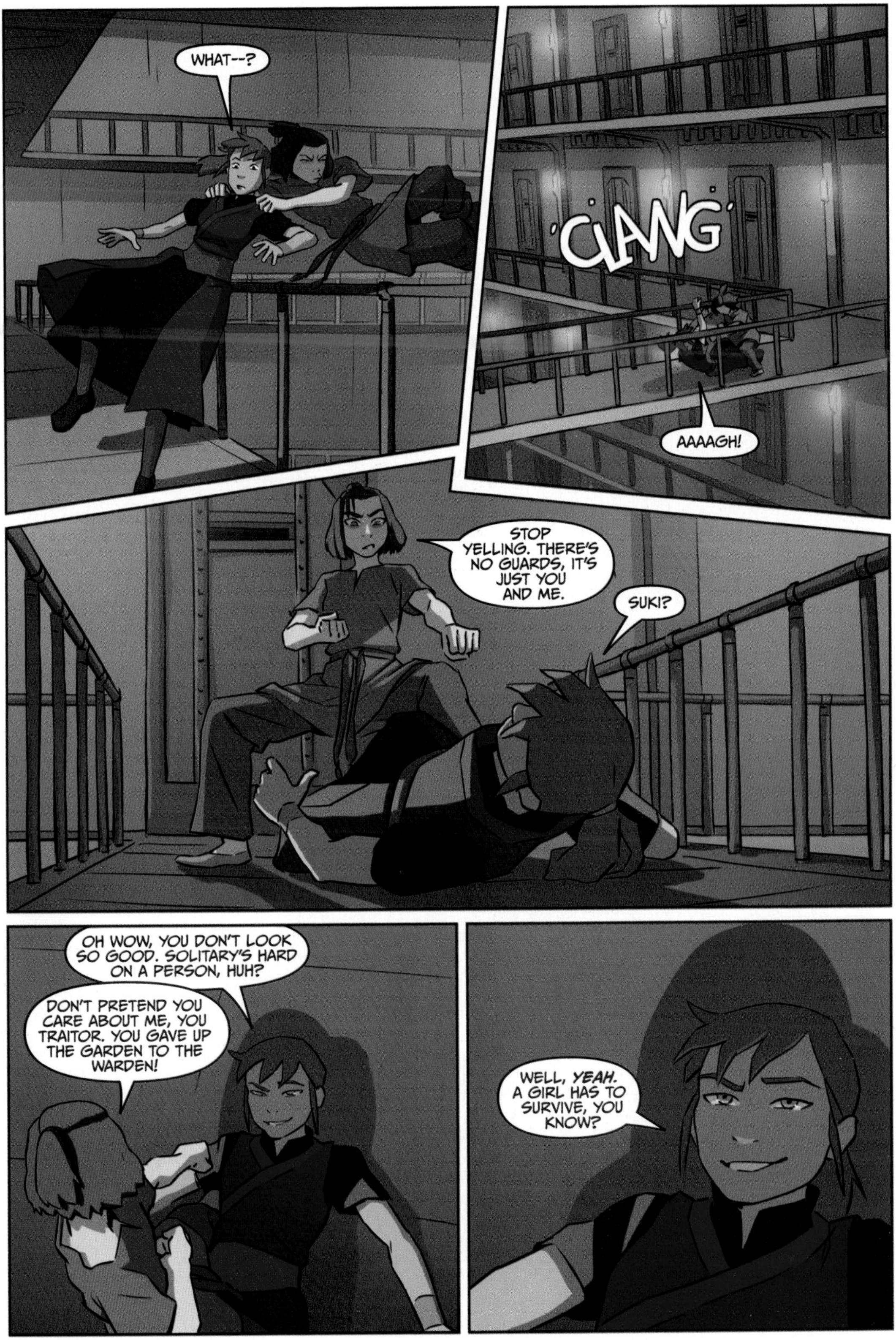
WHAT--?
CLANG
AAAAGH!
STOP YELLING. THERE'S NO GUARDS, IT'S JUST YOU AND ME.
SUKI?
OH WOW, YOU DON'T LOOK SO GOOD. SOLITARY'S HARD ON A PERSON, HUH?
DON'T PRETEND YOU CARE ABOUT ME, YOU TRAITOR. YOU GAVE UP THE GARDEN TO THE WARDEN!
WELL, *YEAH.* A GIRL HAS TO SURVIVE, YOU KNOW?

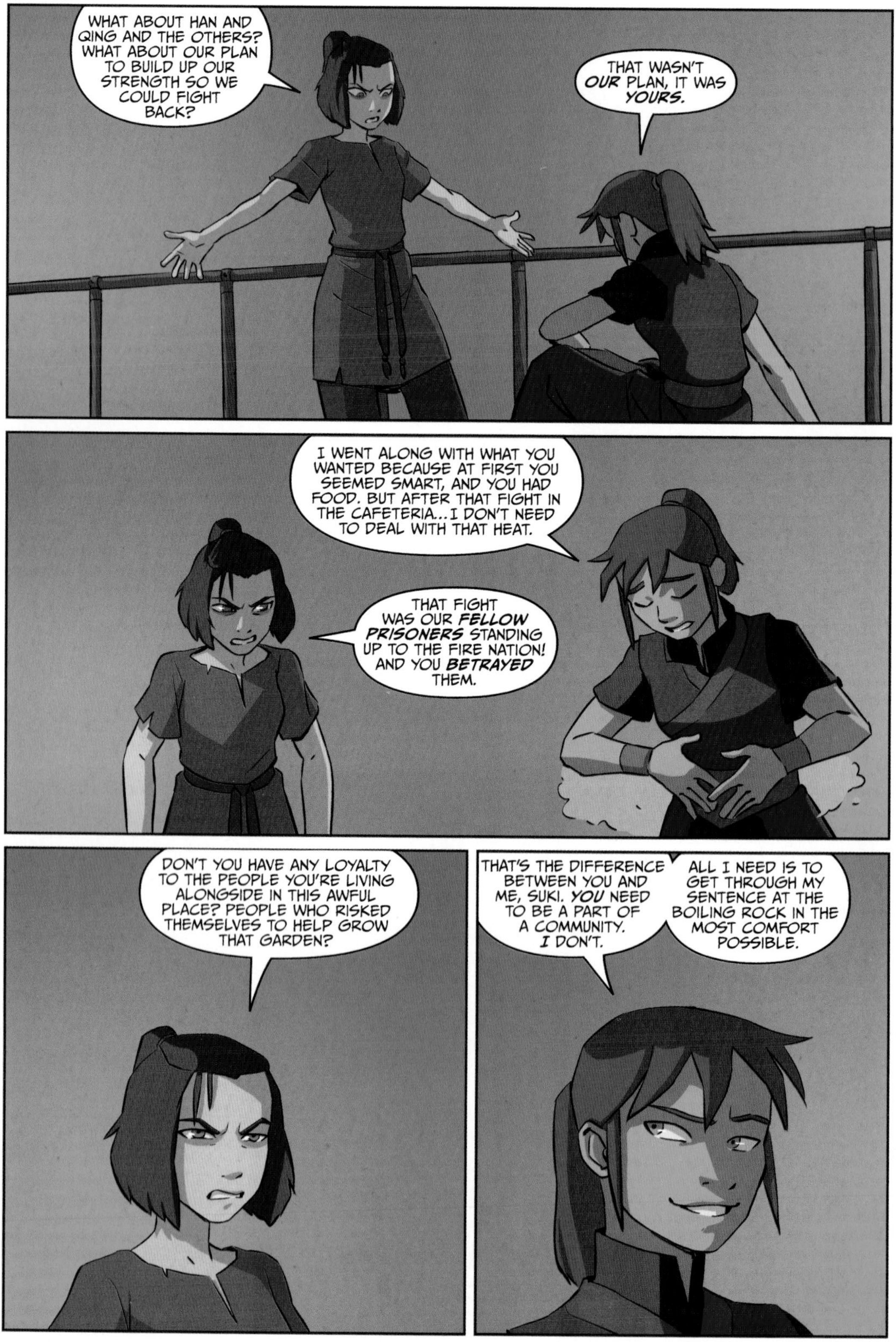
WHAT ABOUT HAN AND QING AND THE OTHERS? WHAT ABOUT OUR PLAN TO BUILD UP OUR STRENGTH SO WE COULD FIGHT BACK?
THAT WASN'T OUR PLAN, IT WAS YOURS.
I WENT ALONG WITH WHAT YOU WANTED BECAUSE AT FIRST YOU SEEMED SMART, AND YOU HAD FOOD. BUT AFTER THAT FIGHT IN THE CAFETERIA...I DON'T NEED TO DEAL WITH THAT HEAT.
THAT FIGHT WAS OUR FELLOW PRISONERS STANDING UP TO THE FIRE NATION! AND YOU BETRAYED THEM.
DON'T YOU HAVE ANY LOYALTY TO THE PEOPLE YOU'RE LIVING ALONGSIDE IN THIS AWFUL PLACE? PEOPLE WHO RISKED THEMSELVES TO HELP GROW THAT GARDEN?
THAT'S THE DIFFERENCE BETWEEN YOU AND ME, SUKI. YOU NEED TO BE A PART OF A COMMUNITY. I DON'T.
ALL I NEED IS TO GET THROUGH MY SENTENCE AT THE BOILING ROCK IN THE MOST COMFORT POSSIBLE.

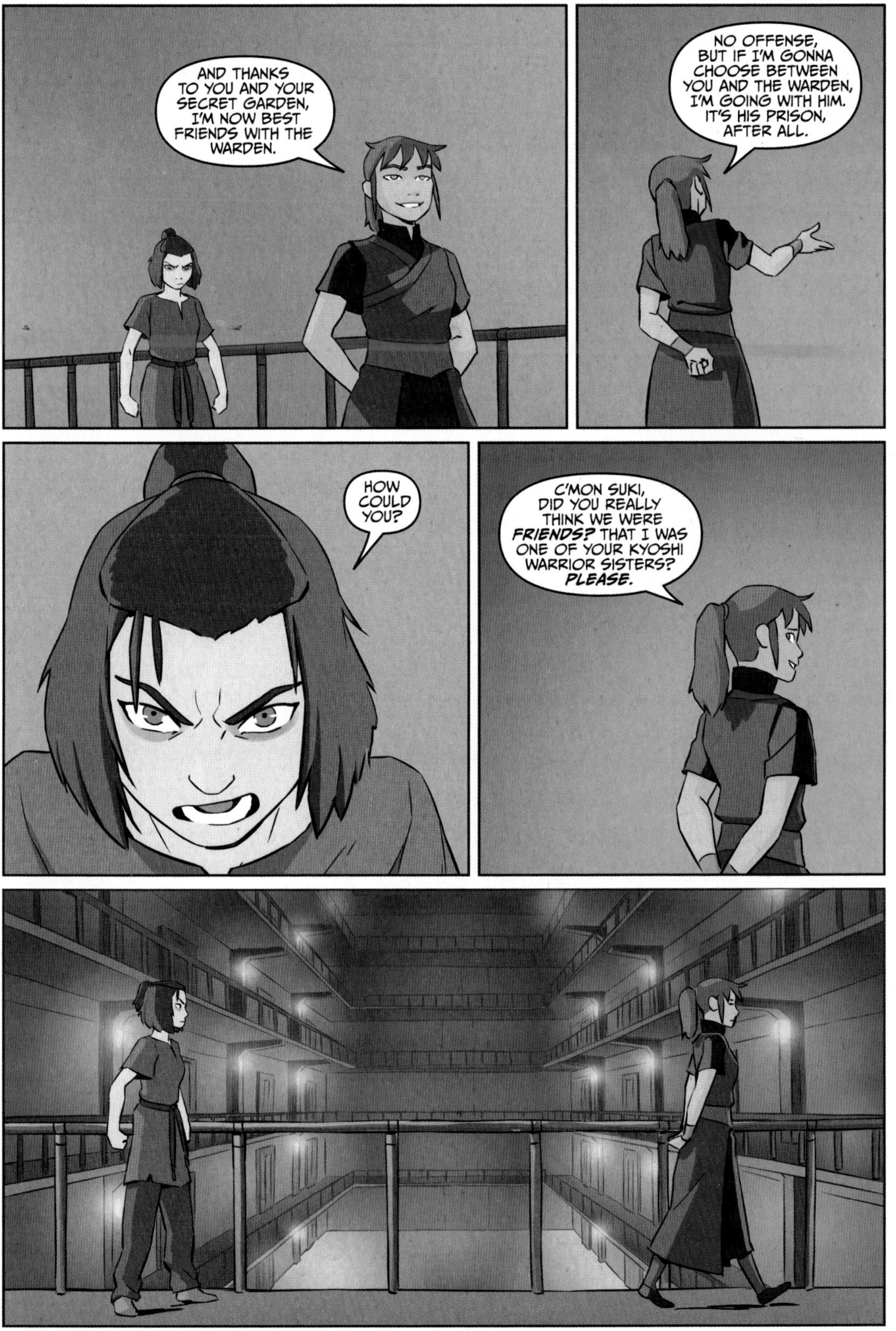
AND THANKS TO YOU AND YOUR SECRET GARDEN, I'M NOW BEST FRIENDS WITH THE WARDEN.
NO OFFENSE, BUT IF I'M GONNA CHOOSE BETWEEN YOU AND THE WARDEN, I'M GOING WITH HIM. IT'S HIS PRISON, AFTER ALL.
HOW COULD YOU?
C'MON SUKI, DID YOU REALLY THINK WE WERE *FRIENDS?* THAT I WAS ONE OF YOUR KYOSHI WARRIOR SISTERS? *PLEASE.*

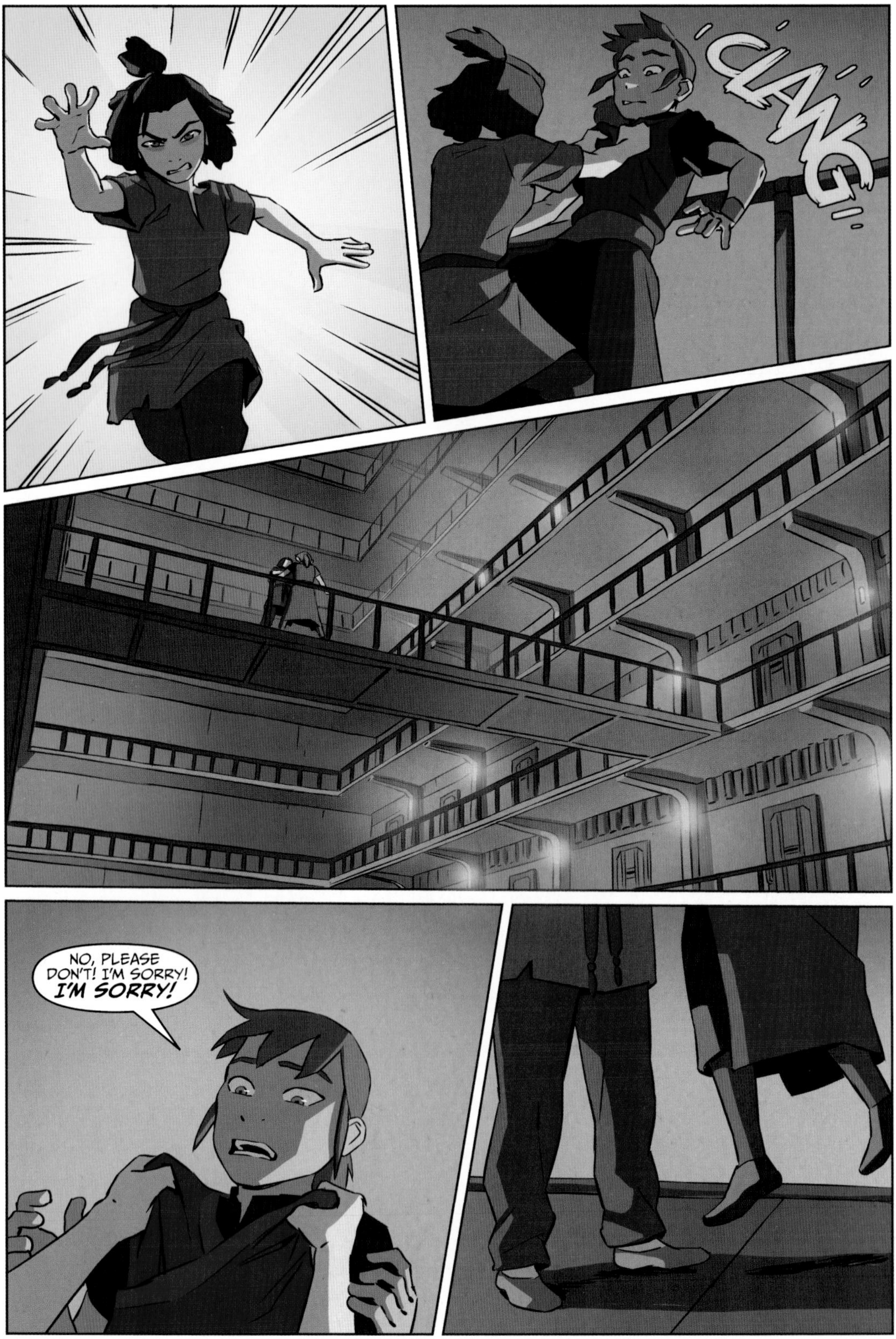
CLANG
NO, PLEASE DON'T! I'M SORRY! I'M SORRY!

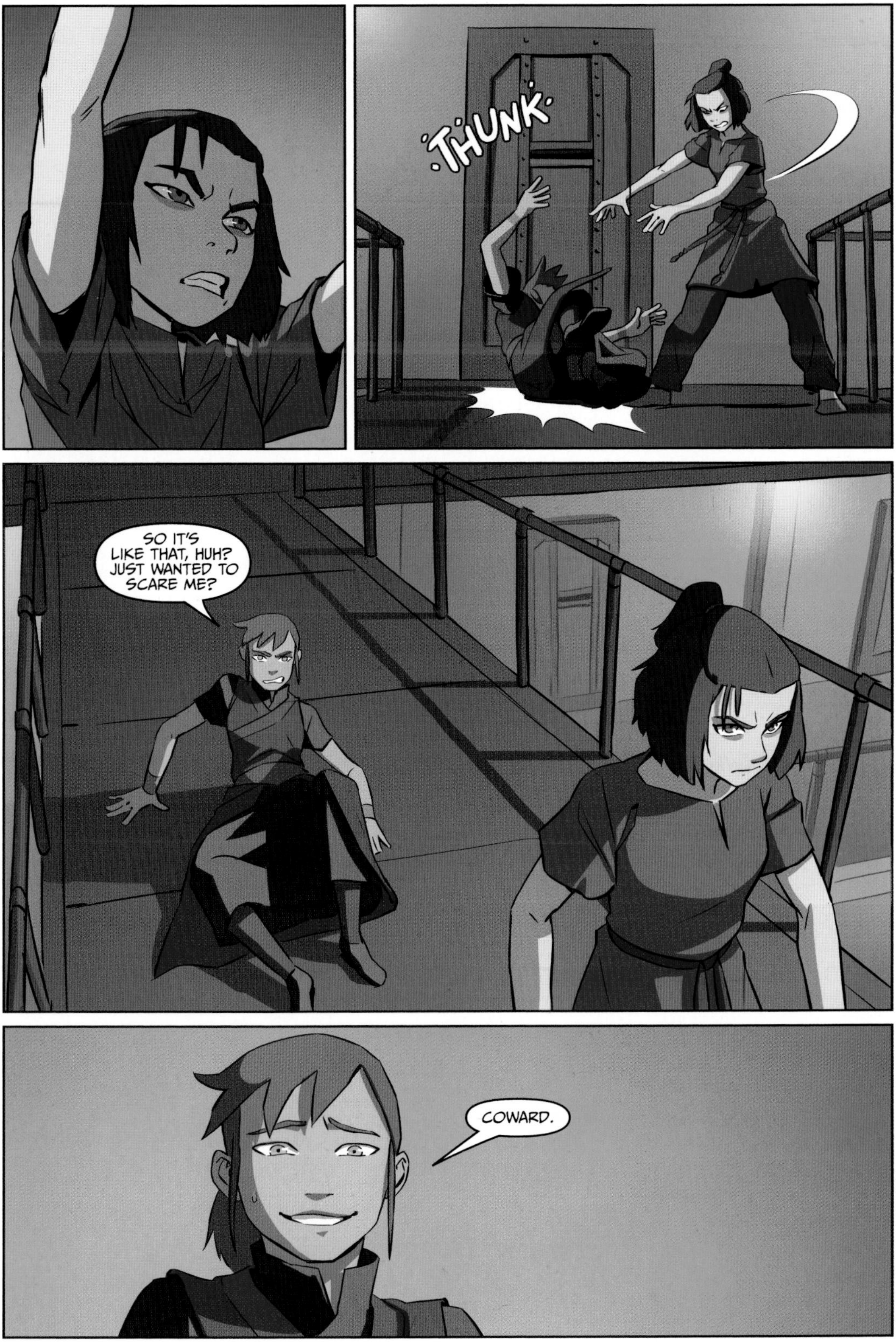
THUNK
SO IT'S LIKE THAT, HUH? JUST WANTED TO SCARE ME?
COWARD.

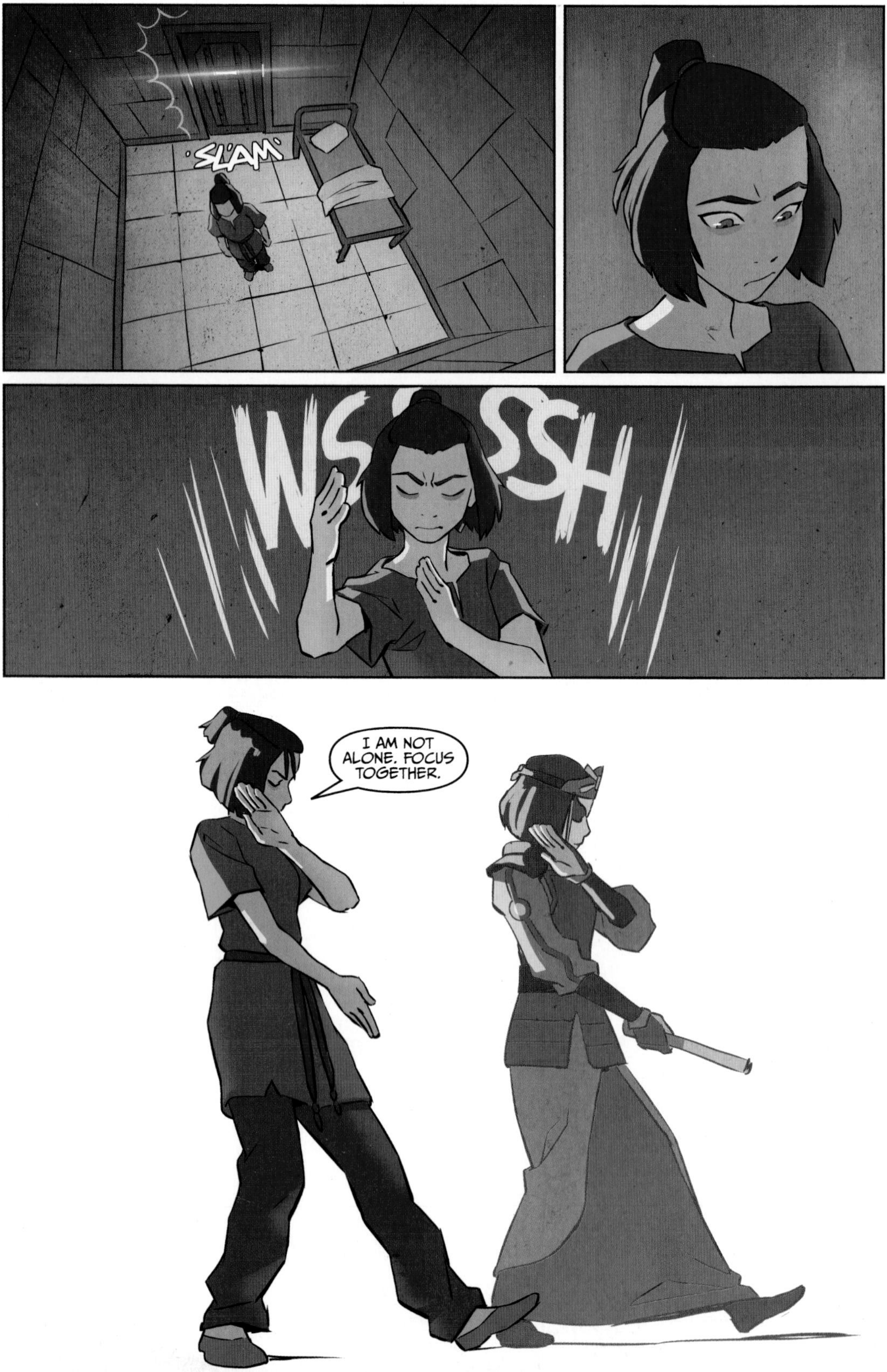
SLAM
I AM NOT ALONE. FOCUS TOGETHER.

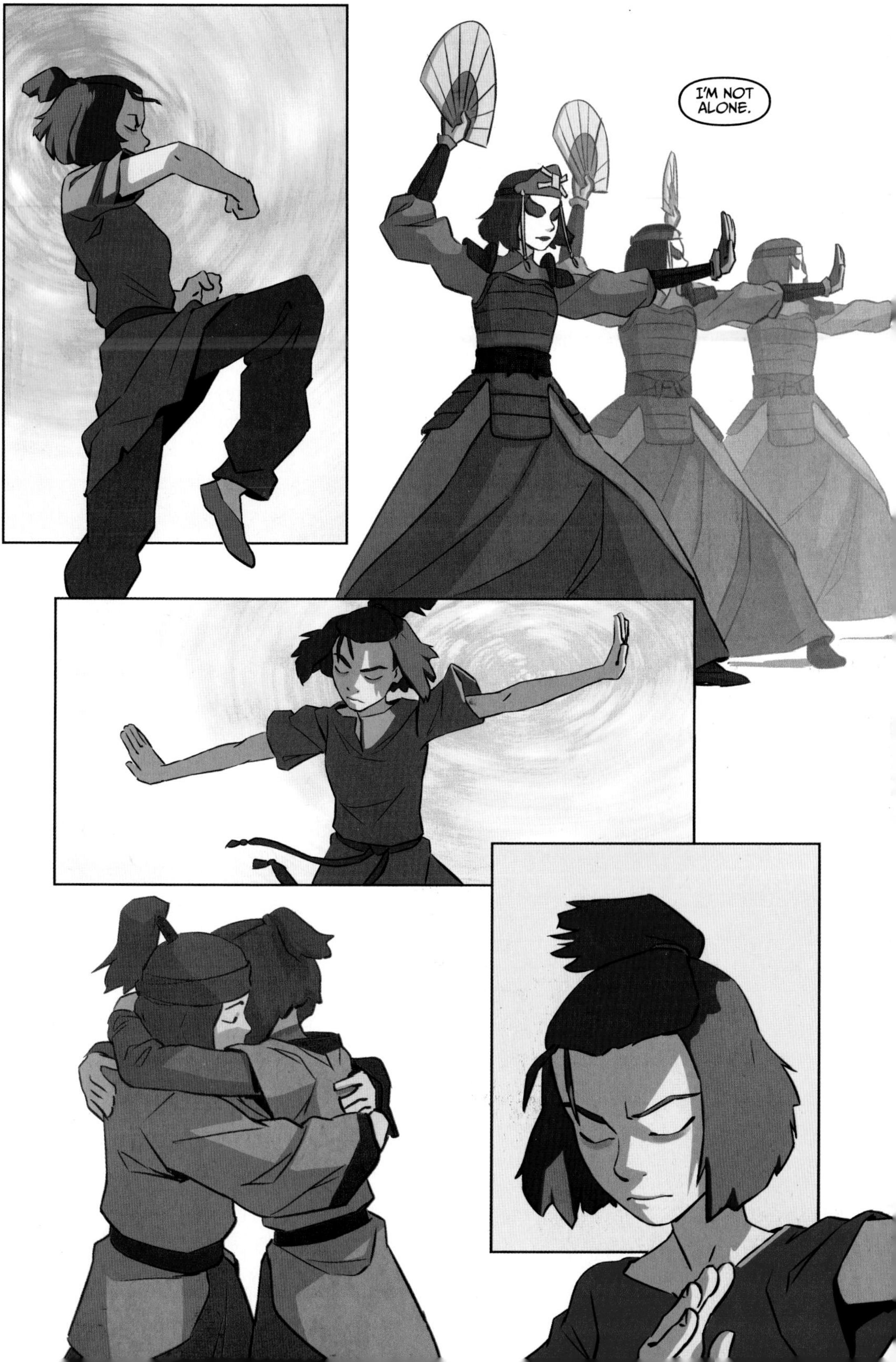
I'M NOT ALONE.

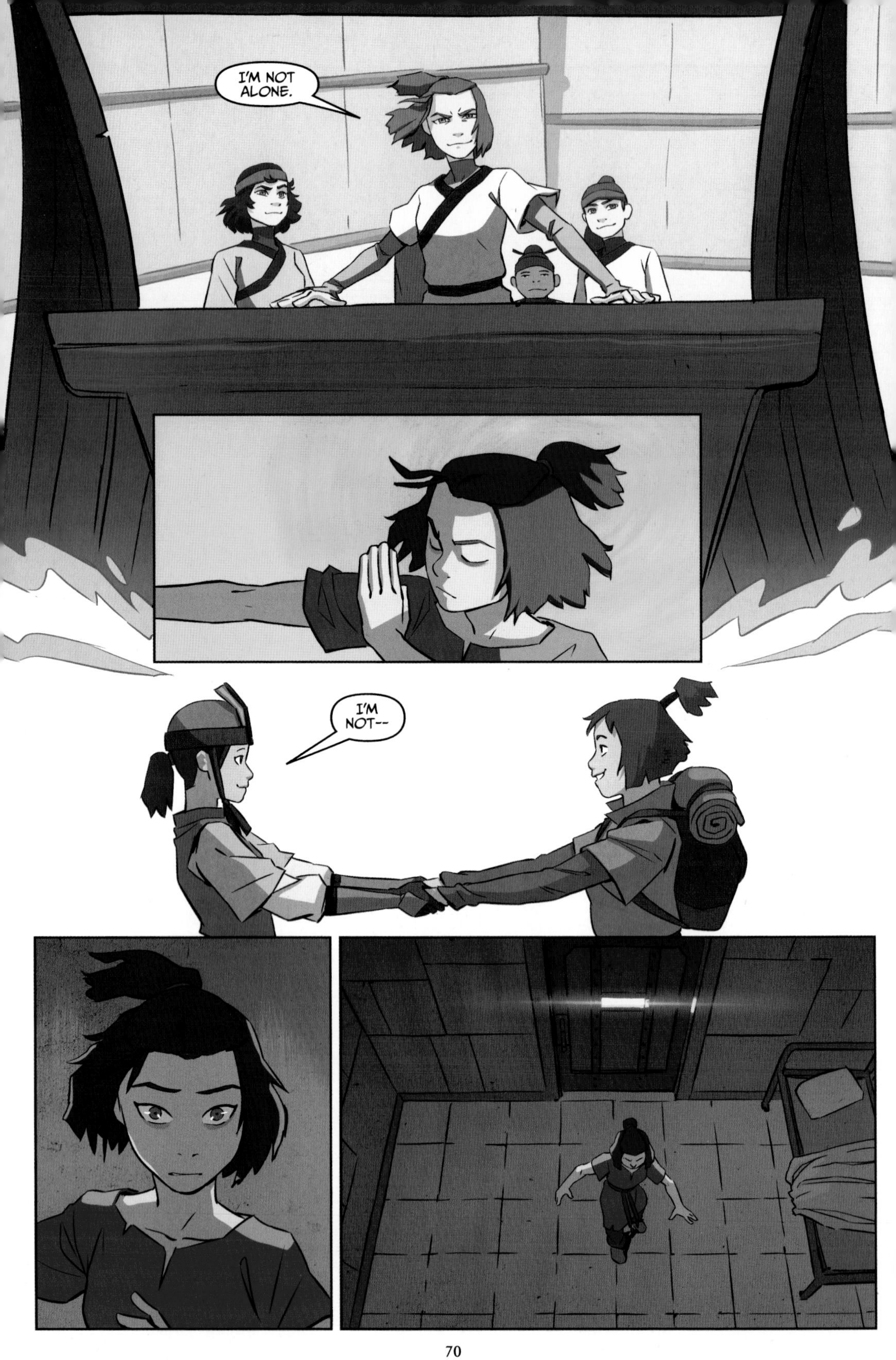
I'M NOT ALONE.
I'M NOT--

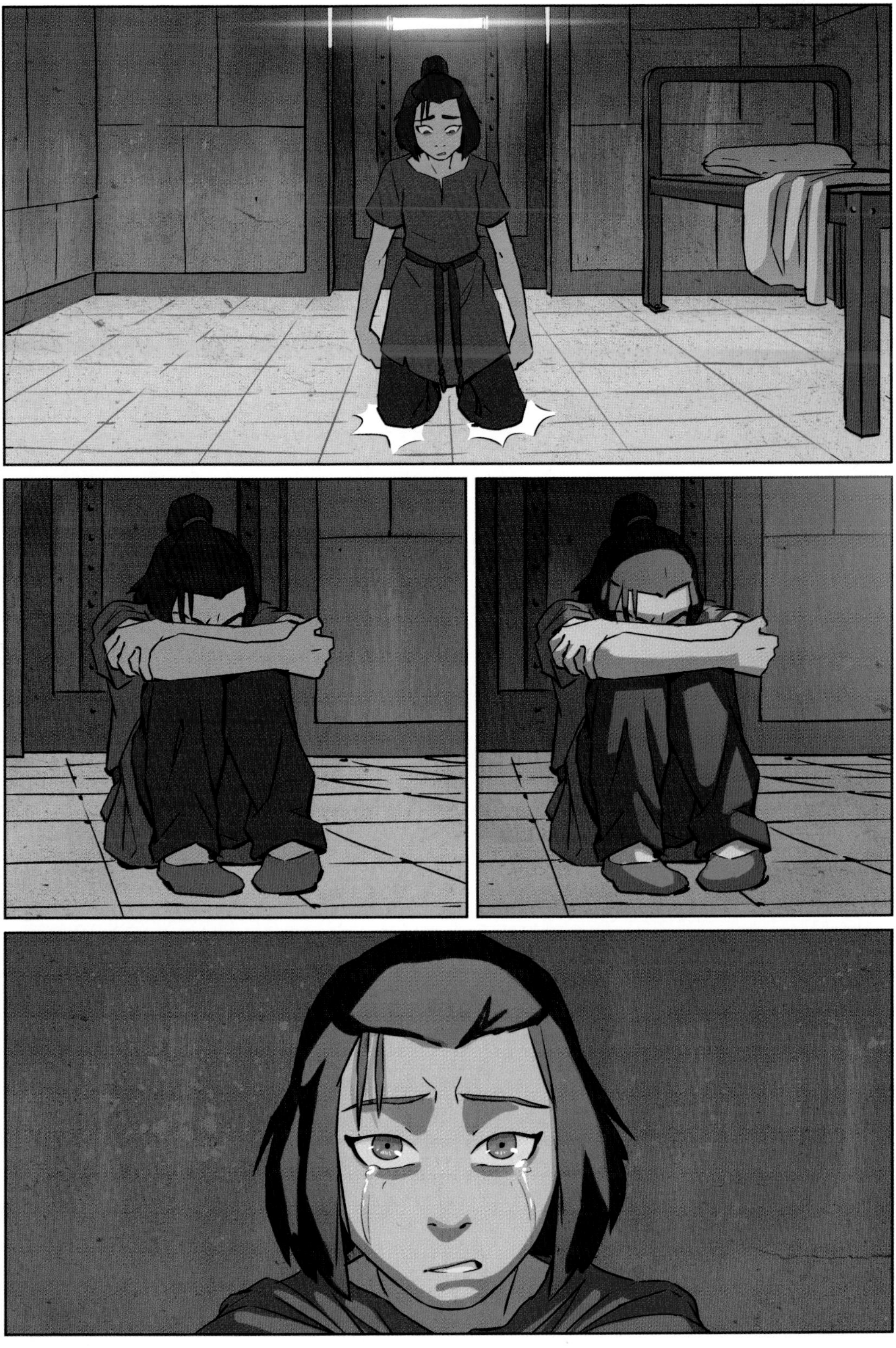

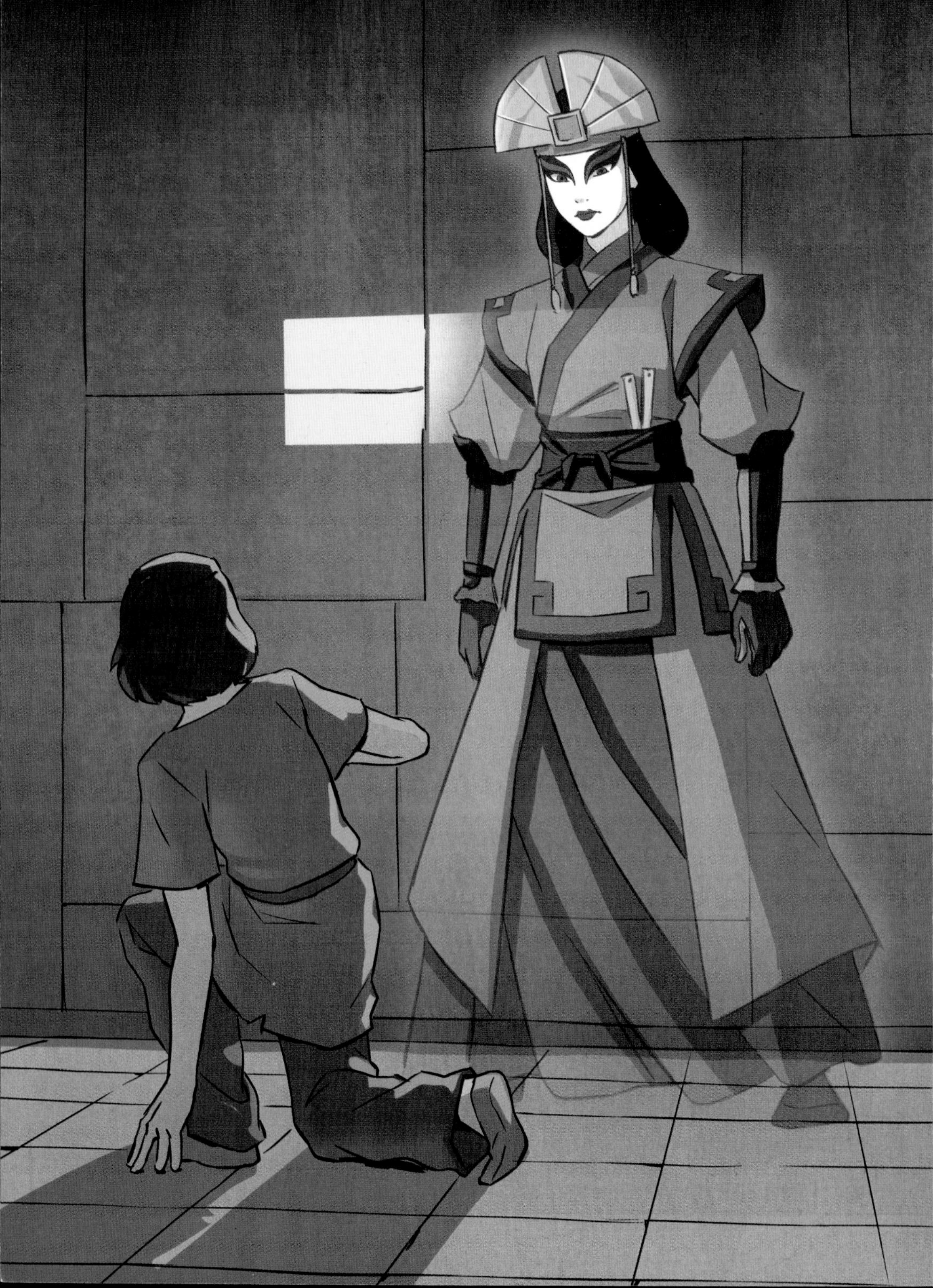

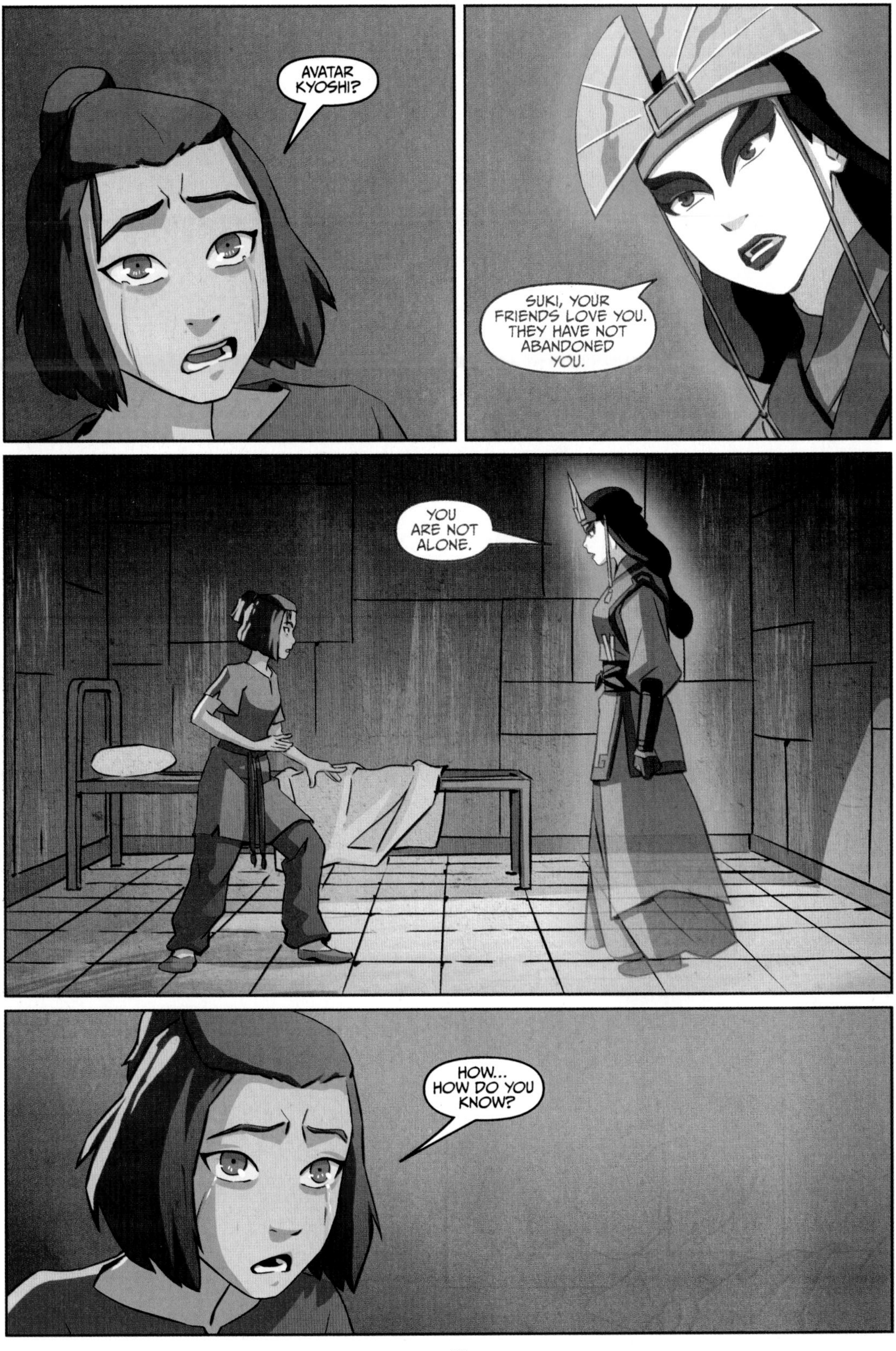
AVATAR KYOSHI?
SUKI, YOUR FRIENDS LOVE YOU. THEY HAVE NOT ABANDONED YOU.
YOU ARE NOT ALONE.
HOW... HOW DO YOU KNOW?

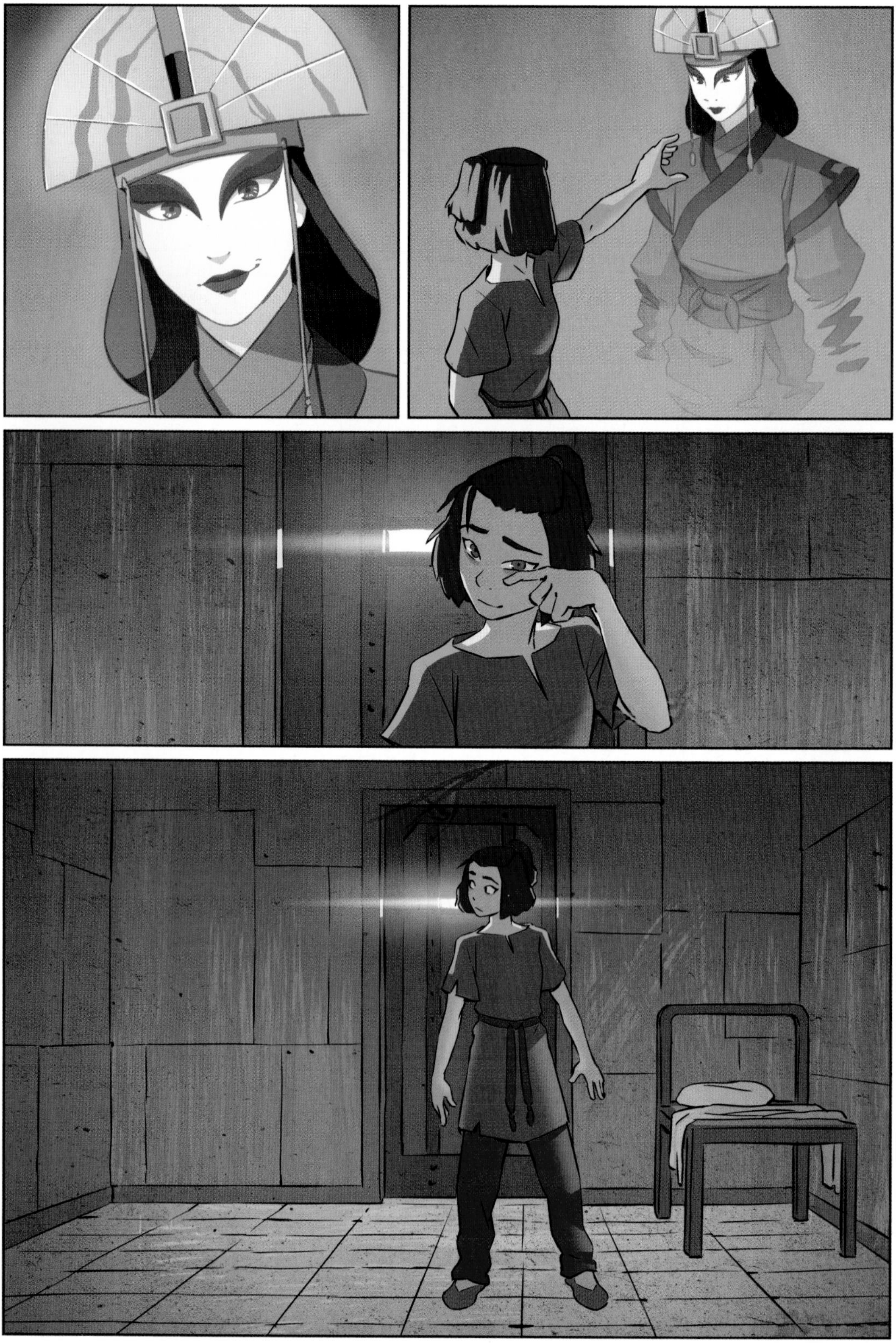

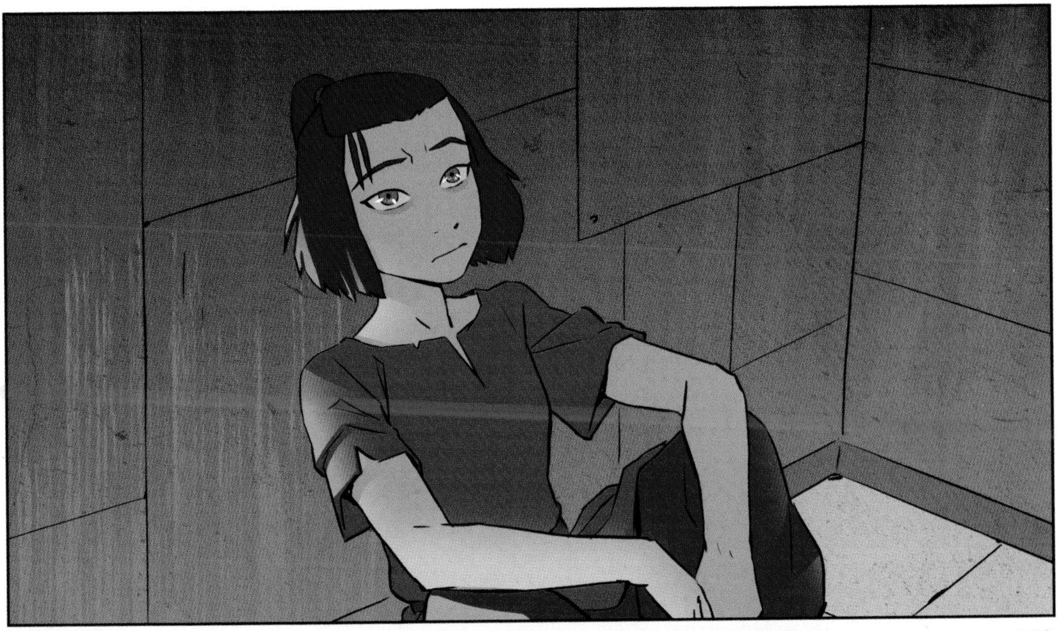
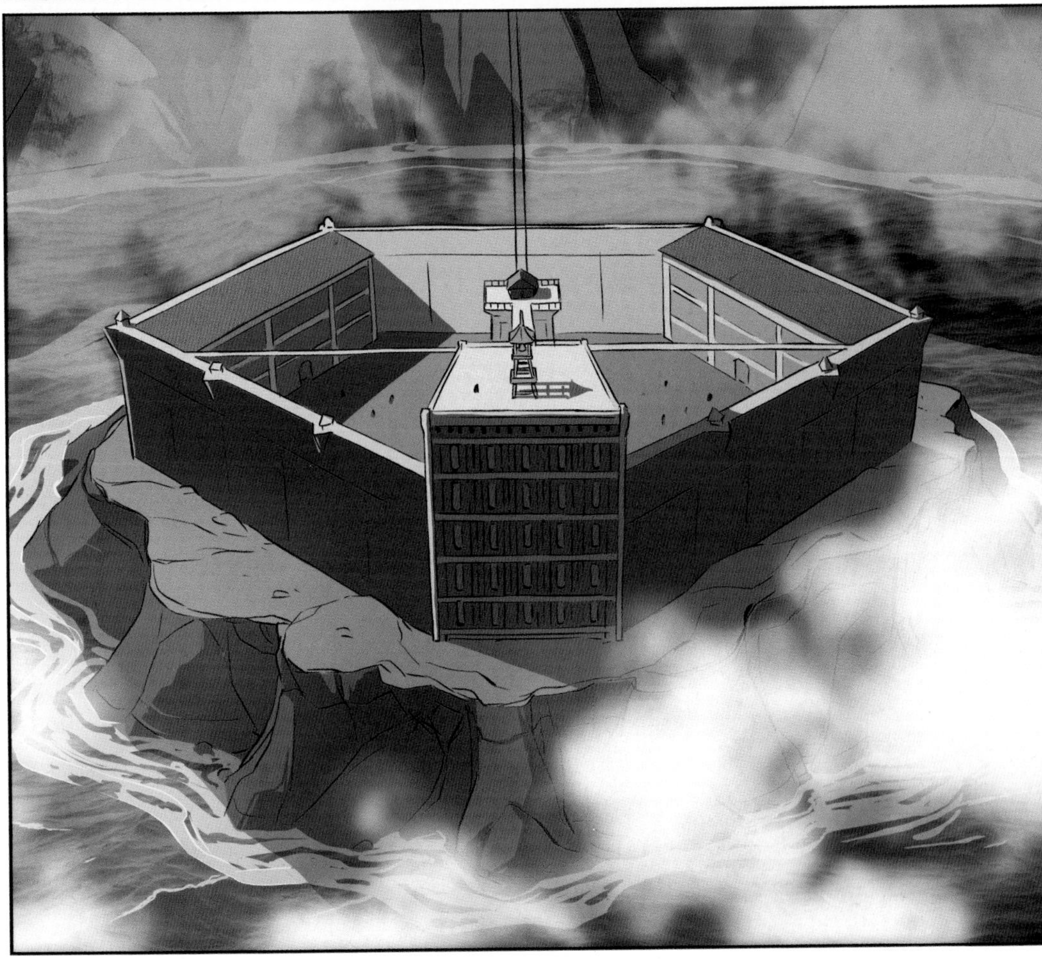

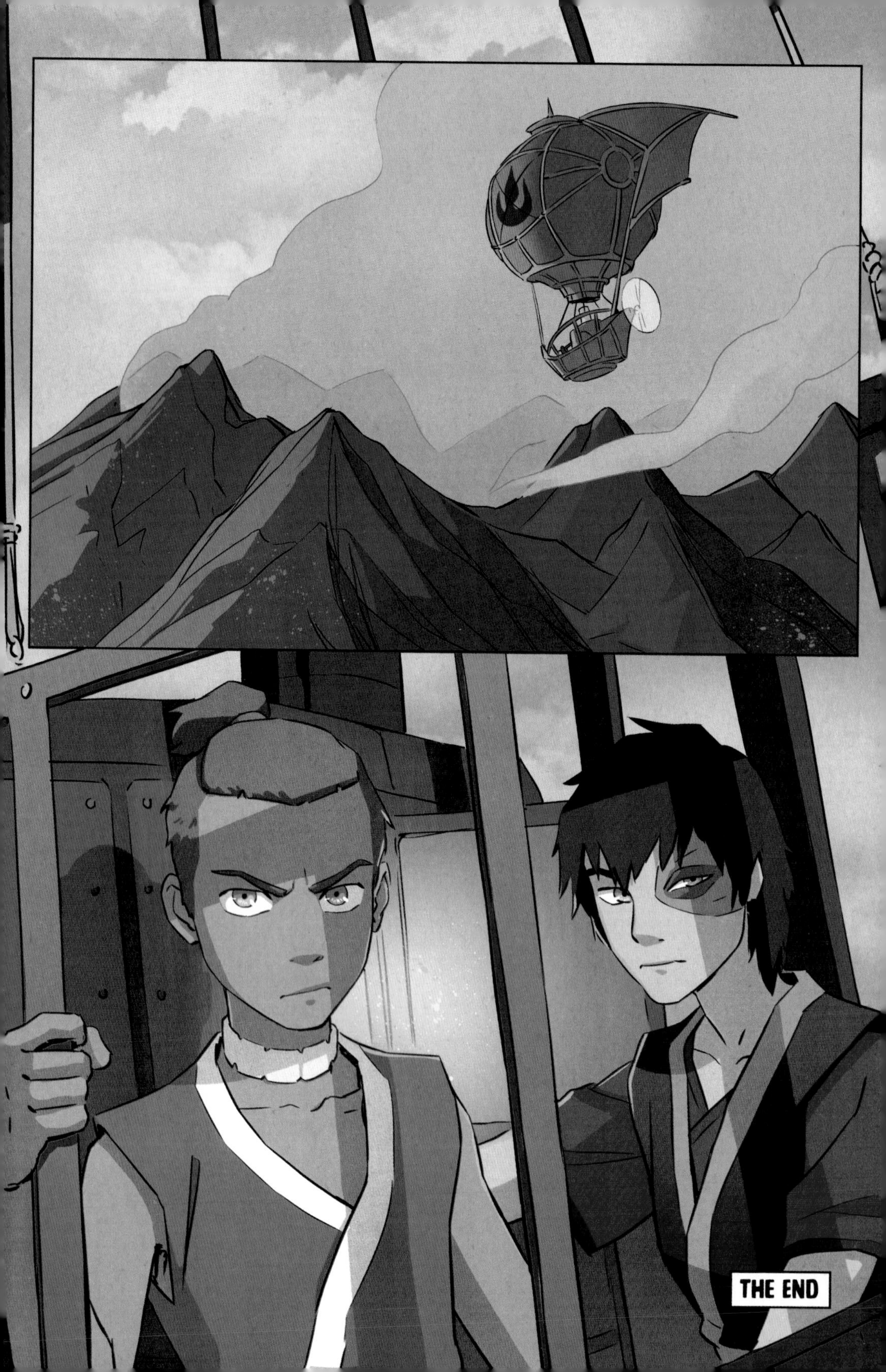
THE END

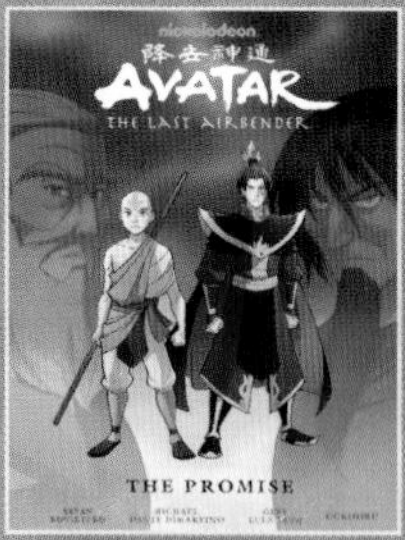
AVATAR
THE LAST AIRBENDER
THE PROMISE

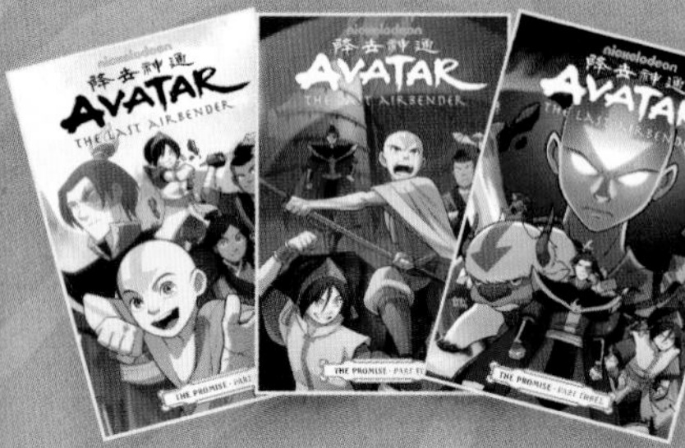
AVATAR
THE LAST AIRBENDER

Avatar: The Last Airbender—The Promise Library Edition
978-1-61655-074-5 $39.99

Avatar: The Last Airbender—The Promise Part 1
978-1-59582-811-8 $12.99

Avatar: The Last Airbender—The Promise Part 2
978-1-59582-875-0 $12.99

Avatar: The Last Airbender—The Promise Part 3
978-1-59582-941-2 $12.99

Avatar: The Last Airbender—The Search Library Edition
978-1-61655-226-8 $39.99

Avatar: The Last Airbender—The Search Part 1
978-1-61655-054-7 $12.99

Avatar: The Last Airbender—The Search Part 2
978-1-61655-190-2 $12.99

Avatar: The Last Airbender—The Search Part 3
978-1-61655-184-1 $12.99

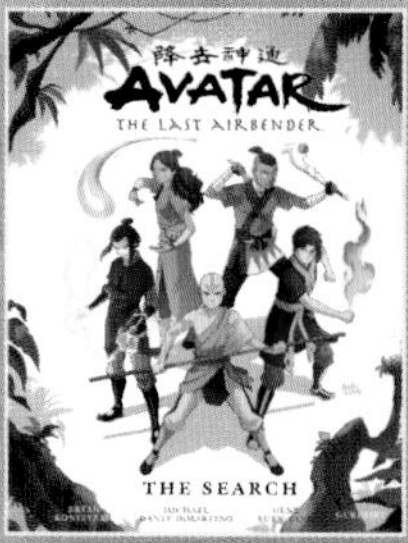
AVATAR
THE LAST AIRBENDER
THE SEARCH

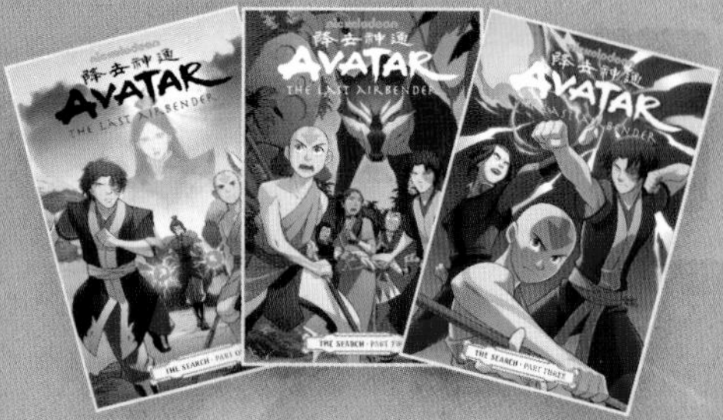
AVATAR

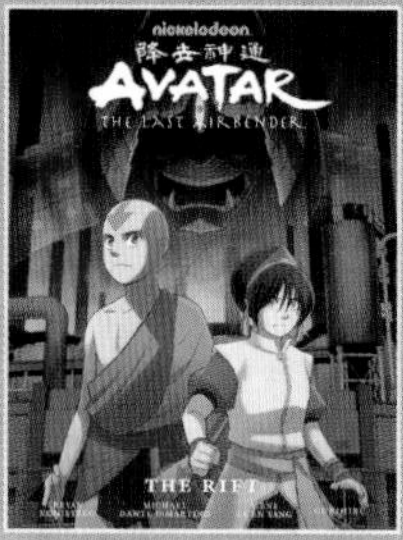
nickelodeon
AVATAR
THE LAST AIRBENDER
THE RIFT

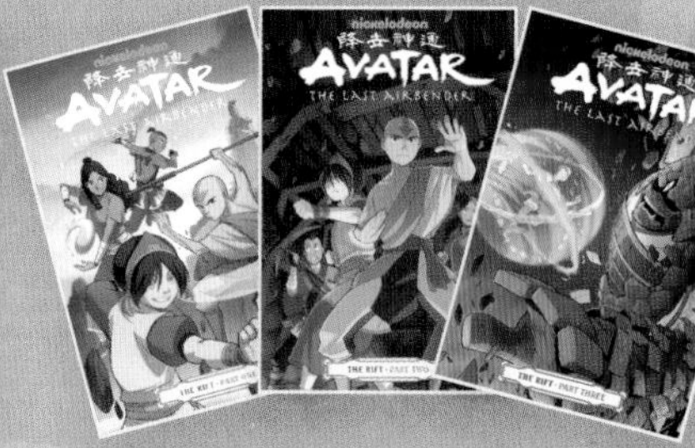
AVATAR

Avatar: The Last Airbender—The Rift Library Edition
978-1-61655-550-4 $39.99

Avatar: The Last Airbender—The Rift Part 1
978-1-61655-295-4 $12.99

Avatar: The Last Airbender—The Rift Part 2
978-1-61655-296-1 $12.99

Avatar: The Last Airbender—The Rift Part 3
978-1-61655-297-8 $12.99

Avatar: The Last Airbender—Smoke and Shadow Library Edition
978-1-50670-013-7 $39.99

Avatar: The Last Airbender—Smoke and Shadow Part 1
978-1-61655-761-4 $12.99

Avatar: The Last Airbender—Smoke and Shadow Part 2
978-1-61655-790-4 $12.99

Avatar: The Last Airbender—Smoke and Shadow Part 3
978-1-61655-838-3 $12.99

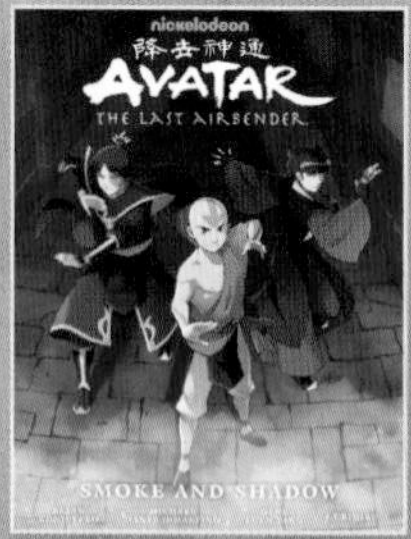
nickelodeon
AVATAR
THE LAST AIRBENDER
SMOKE AND SHADOW

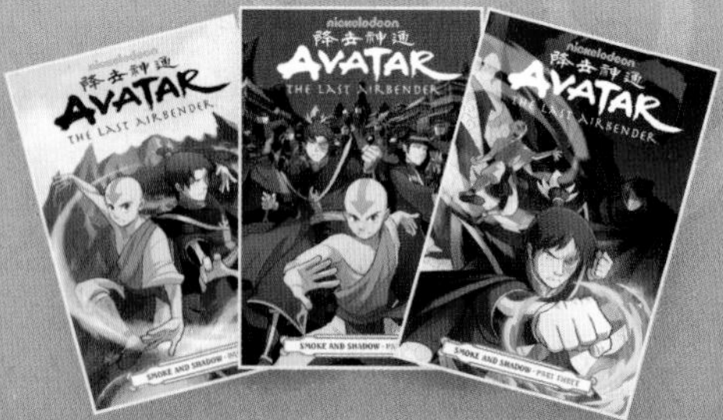
AVATAR
THE LAST AIRBENDER

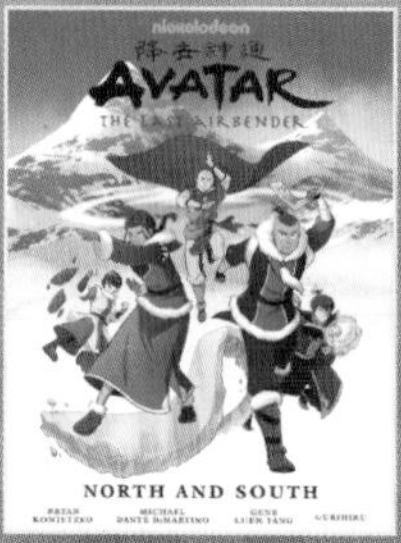
nickelodeon
AVATAR
THE LAST AIRBENDER
NORTH AND SOUTH

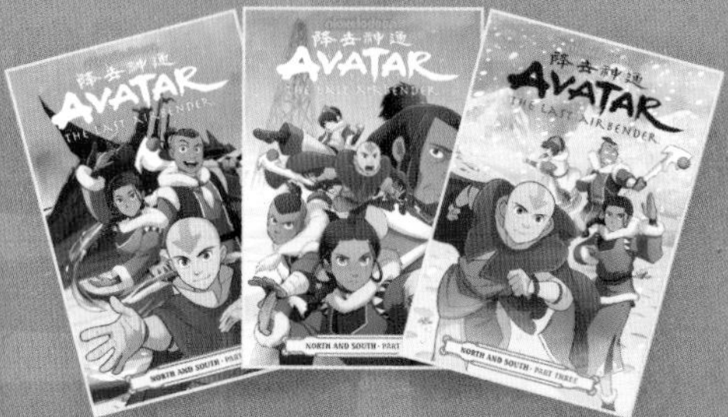
AVATAR
THE LAST AIRBENDER

Avatar: The Last Airbender—North and South Library Edition
978-1-50670-195-0 $39.99

Avatar: The Last Airbender—North and South Part 1
978-1-50670-022-9 $12.99

Avatar: The Last Airbender—North and South Part 2
978-1-50670-129-5 $12.99

Avatar: The Last Airbender—North and South Part 3
978-1-50670-130-1 $12.99